MW00989472

PASTOR AND PARISH

PASTOR AND PARISH
The Psychological Core of Ecclesiastical Conflicts

Robert L. Randall, B.D., Ph.D.

Ministry of Counseling
St. Peter's United Church of Christ
Elmhurst, Illinois

 HUMAN SCIENCES PRESS, INC.

Library of Congress Cataloging-in-Publication Data

Randall, Robert L., 1942–
    Pastor and parish.

    Bibliography: p.
    Includes index.
    1. Church controversies. 2. Clergy—Psychology.
3. Parishes—Psychology. I. Title.
BV652.9.R36 1987   253'.01'9   86-27176
ISBN 0-89885-348-6

CONTENTS

Dedicated to
The Well-being of Pastors and Parishes
and to
The Memory of Heinz Kohut

INTRODUCTION

Rev. David F. quickly detached his hand from mine and without a word preceded his anxious-looking wife into my office. His manner was consistent with the message he had given me over the phone when calling for a counseling appointment—he didn't want to come, and he was angry. In spite of his resistance, he was quite verbal about his outrage. In good faith he had accepted a call to a small-town congregation. The people there had seemed glad about it. The position had looked full of promise for himself and for his family as well. This parish, he anticipated, would be a thankful contrast to the last church he had served in the city.

That inner-city congregation had not appreciated him. They had failed to give him the respect he considered his due as their pastor. When he had tried to assert leadership and bring about change, for example, his efforts and plans were rejected by the consistory. Furthermore, parishioners failed to attend worship on a committed, regular basis, which he also took as a personal affront. A small-town church would be different, as he had envisioned it. They would embrace him with the kind of attentiveness appropriate for himself as their minister.

Three months later his soothing fantasies were decimated. The congregation quickly became critical of his style of ministry, constantly comparing him unfavorably with the socially visible and successful pastor of the large, elite church in town. Support for his ministry eroded, then vanished, leaving him personally and professionally isolated. To make matters even more painful, the first words of the big church pastor to this newly arrived colleague were: "Let me say at the start that we outnumber you two to one."

Rev. David F. was crushed. Again he felt belittled, unappreciated. Along with sleepless nights, he experienced chest pains. Suicidal thoughts entered his mind with disturbing ease and acceptance. He distanced himself increasingly from parishioners. Nothing his wife did pleased him. The children irritated him so much that he didn't want them around.

Thought patterns regressed to primary levels. No matter how long-suffering and supportive his wife was, for example, he insisted she loved her family more than she loved him. Rational boundaries gave way to engulfing generalizations: he didn't just hate this church, he hated churches; he wasn't hostile toward just the pompous "big church" pastor in town, or toward conference officials (who failed to set the small-town church straight); he was hostile toward *all* ministers, including, sight unseen, this pastoral psychotherapist to whom he was reluctantly talking. And when this pastoral psychotherapist, after expressing understanding of how devastating the churches' responses had been to him, then tried, with great gentleness, to suggest that his intense reactions were possibly touched off as well by other struggles he had inside his self, David nearly stormed out of the office.

The small-town church itself was full of its own rage-filled reactions to real and inferred assaults on its character. Much of its group energy over the years had been given to a relentless preoccupation about being second-best. Any comparison of them by outsiders to the "big church" elicited their outrage, and yet they as a group constantly used the big church as the model for what they were not, yet could become. In this state of injured self-esteem and resulting anger, they looked for a pastor who, by his own grandeur, his own sparkling, community-oriented personality, could rival the pompous pastor of the big church and finally lift them up as a congregation into that aura of community envy and admiration they so intensely desired—and demanded. Not only had Rev. David F. failed to fulfill this mission; he was a further humiliation to them in the community.

Hope, goodwill, and empathy between the pastor and parish quickly dissolved. In this severely stressed state of mutually mortified selves, where both minister and congregation were disintegrating emotionally, physically, cognitively, and spiritually, an escalating pattern of retaliation for injuries suffered ensued. At its height, the council voted to reduce their pastor's already minimal salary, while yet demanding that he carry out a full range of church duties if he wanted to stay. In his fury at these continuing insults, David let all the faucets in the parsonage flow full force at night in order to drive up the church's water and heating bills. Both pastor and parish were falling apart in their own ways, but neither would bend from their righteously considered position of being the party to whom reparation should be made.

THE TERRAIN OF PASTOR AND PARISH STRUGGLES

Rev. David F. and the "second-best" church are struggling, with their own self and with each other. On one level we expect it. "Difficulties of ministers and congregations come with the territory," quipped one weathered, but not beaten, denominational leader. Ministers through the generations have commonly reported being burned up at their congregations, burned out spiritually, and bothered by marital problems. Congregations have chronicled difficulties retaining members, staying solvent, and getting along with pastors. At the same time, however, we who care for the church and empathize with pastors hurt when they hurt; and our concern intensifies when we suspect that the terrain may be getting rougher. Conversations with denominational leaders and pastoral counselors suggest that there is an increase in the proportion of pastors and parishes who are suffering.

"In my 30 years as a conference minister, I cannot recall a time when there were so many hurting ministers and congregations out there," lamented one sensitive pastor to pastors. A denominationally appointed pastoral counselor observed, "There are more pastors in our churches who need psychiatric hospitalization or could be certified for hospitalization than ever before." In addition to this, these parish-pastor problems appear more severe, persistent, and devastating in effect. An intensity explosion may be accompanying the numbers explosion.

Whether old or altered, the struggles exist. Many of us pastors and congregations know them too personally. My effort in these following pages is to clarify a primary and powerful dynamic underlying these struggles, struggles that exist on a wide spectrum: from those of a severely destructive nature, such as with Rev. David F. and the "second-best" church, to those characterized by mildly pervasive irritations and disappointments. Based on my years of pastoral and clinical psychotherapy with ministers and their families, and on close, involved analysis of church life, I, along with colleagues, have come to understand that *the loss of personal and spiritual cohesion in pastors and parishes is psychologically rooted in the injuries to and weaknesses in their "self."*

Conversely and broadly stated, healing and restoring power emanates from those pastors and parishes whose selves are experienced as cohesive, vital, and harmonious. A healthy self is that essential psychological base from which pastors and parishes are able to reach out marvelously beyond their own views and hurts with an embracing empathy for others that is of salvation's very essence. A self riddled with vulnerabilities is that psychological base from which pastors and parishes are unable to experience and convey the *grace* they have supposedly received.

The structure and dynamics of these self struggles—in pastors and parishes individually and in their interactions—can best be understood from a body of psychological reflection known as "self psychology." "Self psychology" is the name by which the seminal insights of Heinz Kohut and other like-minded colleagues have come to be known in the areas of psychoanalysis, psychology, and pastoral counseling. From his work as a psychoanalyst, Kohut gradually discovered that at the center of our psychological life are certain self needs. These self needs are referred to as "narcissistic needs." Before Kohut, these narcissistic needs were only vaguely understood. Kohut's work with people suffering from narcissistic disorders (self disorders) brought conceptual and therapeutic clarity into this critical domain of narcissism and narcissistic needs, and resulted in the development of a new psychological paradigm and approach called "self psychology." We shall discuss this further in Chapter 2.

The debilitation of Protestant pastors I have worked with, and the decay of Protestant parishes which I have served as a consultant or have known, primarily derive from underlying difficulties in what normally should be a healthily developed self of each. These difficulties represent "narcissistic struggles of pastors and parishes." This was the case with Rev. D. S. and the second-best church. Chronic weaknesses in the cohesiveness of their selves, vulnerable self-esteem, and tendencies to respond with degrees of despair and rage when their pressing narcissistic needs/demands were not responded to, disabled a community called together by God and a pastor called to be a means of grace.

Unfortunately, this scenario is, as has been noted, not an isolated one. Many pastors and parishes are struggling. *The intensity, persistence, and character of the unmet narcissistic needs shape the pattern and depth of parish-pastor problems, and ultimately influence the very survival of churches and ministers.* Our focus will be upon these narcissistic strivings as they manifest themselves in the individual lives of pastors (Chapter 3), in the group lives of parishes (Chapter 4), and upon the particular patterns of struggle that arise when the narcissistic needs of a pastor and a parish meet head on, as they inevitably do (Chapter 5). Finally, in our last chapter we will explore how empathy is the grace of God by which struggling pastors and parishes are psychologically redeemed (Chapter 6).

Longings for Empathic Understanding

Pastors and parishes are very dear to me. As a pastoral psychotherapist I am a pastor, and I work and worship within the comforting confines of a parish. There is much in pastor-parish life that truly reflects God's creative and healing grace, that wonderfully reflects the highest expressions of our narcissistic nature: empathy, creativity, a sense of participation in a supraindividual and timeless existence, humor, and wisdom. But we ache when we see pastors and parishes hurt, and when we observe how, from that hurt, they injure others. You and I are not above it all, of course. All of us stand vulnerable. All of us, ministers and churches alike, suffer injuries to our self-esteem, become uncertain about ourselves, sense that we are losing our grip, and then respond with varying degrees of rage and/or depressive withdrawal. *When these things happen to us, our less than nurturing responses erupt from the disintegration of our self's cohesion, rather than from a bedrock of malicious intent.* Those who outwardly hurt others are inwardly hurting.

Our souls cry out for someone empathically to understand this about us! Admonishments and condemnations fail to soothe the hurt or heal the injury, for they do not sufficiently touch our wound's emotional center. The context in which we preach and teach and counsel is a world of tragically sensitive and uncertain selves. We, too, are the patient. The laments of pastors I hear in my counseling office are not so much of guilt, but of emptiness; not so much fear of punishment, but fear of being ridiculed, ignored, forgotten; not so much dread of physical death, but the dread of meaningless days. The struggling pastors I see reach out for those who understand and uplift, rather than for those who judge and exhort.

Our hope for restoration comes from being surrounded by this spirit of empathic understanding (Chapter 6). Only in this empathic milieu can we slowly begin, once again, to expose our self, to risk a glimpse from behind our resistive walls and effectively encounter the past pain, the persistent archaic narcissistic wishes, and the vulnerabilities of our self. Healing empathy is both expressed and broadened when we come to accept the legitimate narcissistic needs within our self and in the selves of others, and when we come to understand the disturbing responses of our self and the selves of others when these needs are thwarted. In so doing, we pastors and parishes move toward a state of holy wholeness, fulfilling the promise given us that we might have life, and have it abundantly. This book hopes to be a companion-guide on that journey as it attempts to illuminate the ecclesiastical relationship in a new way through the perspective of self psychology.

Chapter 1

THE "SELF" OF PASTOR AND OF PARISH

What is this "self" of pastor and parish we have been alluding to? We can point to this reality by beginning with broad, descriptive statements close to our lived experience. As you sit reading these words, it would be peculiar (we hope) for you to say or acutely experience: "I am these hands holding this book; I am these eyes scanning these pages." As individuals we exist through our body, of course, but we sense being "more" than our body parts or processes. Likewise, in a healthy state you would not tend to experience: "I am these thoughts going on in my head right now," or "I am these mental processes." Similarly, in normal living you do not exist in a state of depersonalization where "all I am is the role that I play."

In contrast to these actually regressive experiences, you implicitly know that there is a more inclusive dimension of you, something that transcends all the "parts" and thus constitutes a kind of "core" of your being. We typically refer to this core as "I," that subjective experience of our total personhood. More commonly, we call this "I," this core of being, our "self." At times each of us is cognizant of being "aware of my self," or we feel painfully "uncertain about my self." When tragedies occur in our lives, we tend to say, "I feel like I'm losing a grip on my self." If, however, we are surprised by an occasion where people celebrate our accomplishments, we tend to say, "I really feel good about my self!" It is accurate here to write "my self" instead of the reflective pronoun "myself," because what is being referred to in our statements is our "self" as the central dimension of our existence, rather than just "myself" as a figure in distinction from others. The point is that, prereflectively, without any rationalistic attempts to prove it, we know that we are a "self," that our self seems to be that depth and wholeness that we are, and that the assuredness and well-being of our self is subject to marked fluctuations.

Self psychology focuses clinically upon the nature and development of this "self" that we are and know implicitly. By empathically entering into the self-experience of others, as well as by utilizing his own self-introspections, Kohut, along with involved colleagues, came to a depth understanding of the self. From a psychology of the self perspective, the self is understood to be our psychic center, i.e., the center of our psychological world. Stated more dynamically, the self is the core of the personality, the nucleus of initiative for the unfolding of an individual's unique ambitions and purposes, skills, and talents, ideals and values.

While these descriptions are accurate, they may be mistakenly interpreted as meaning that the self is just a part of our total psychological makeup, albeit a crucial part. To consider the self as a "part" of our mental or psychic being, however, would be to understand the self only in a narrow way. Kohut helped us grasp the more inclusive reality of the self. The self as the *center* of our psychological world means that the self and its structure is *the psychological bedrock* upon which all our psychosocial cognitive developments are based. All that we are is rooted in this psychological bedrock of our self.

Understood in this way, therefore, the self is not a unity that developed by the gradual integration of diverse psychosocial, biological, or cognitive processes and drives. Instead, even in the child, there is a developing rudimentary self that functions for the healthy integration of complex developing drives and processes. This means that the self is not composed of certain "content" that can be inflexibly defined. Kohut often stated that the self is ultimately undefinable, for the self is *the* psychological bedrock of our being, upon which all that we are is founded. Nevertheless, the self does have structure, and there are developmental requirements for the development of a healthy self, namely, adequate responses to the self's narcissistic needs. Illuminating the structure and development of the self was Kohut's first major contribution to understanding the self from a depth psychological perspective.

Quite clearly, this way of viewing the self contrasts with sociological interpretations of the self. From the framework of self psychology, the self is not to be equated with "identity," for example. The self is not the result of nor the integration of various identities socially learned and acquired. Instead, the self as the psychological core of our being is the basis by which a person is more or less successful in forging and sustaining any identity at all. "Identity crises," therefore, may well arise from underlying difficulties in the structure and development of the person's self. As our inner psychic core, the nature of the self shapes all dimensions of our actions, feelings, beliefs, and roles, but is not defined by them.

The health of the self, as a result, is a quintessential factor determining a person's total state of being and well-being. An individual may experience his self as firm and consistent through time, endowed with positive and reliable self-esteem, and functionally balanced and harmonious. Another individual may experience his self as shaky and always on the verge of falling apart, negatively colored, and organizationally enfeebled. The first self has healthy "self-cohesion." The second self is weakly structured and tends to "fragment" (it lacks reliable self-cohesion). There are varying degrees and types of self-cohesiveness, which are determined in large measure by the history of responses to the self's narcissistic requirements. Self psychology attempts to explicate the process by which the self is more or less successful in forging reliable self-cohesion. Although we will discuss it more thoroughly in our next chapter, the next few pages highlight what determines adequate or inadequate self-development.

HEALTHY AND DEFECTIVE SELF-DEVELOPMENT

The primary self psychology insight is this: There is no development of the self at all without a milieu of empathically responding others (called "selfobjects"), who understandingly give themselves to the narcissistic needs and expectations of the self. Selfobjects are those who the self experiences as part of the self itself, as extensions of the self (hence the term "selfobject"), whose various empathic ministrations the self needs for its development and maintenance. If a child is to survive psychologically, he must be born into an adequately empathic, human selfobject atmosphere, just as a child to survive physically must be born into an adequately oxygenated environmental atmosphere. Both the supportive selfobject atmosphere for the self's narcissistic needs, and the sustaining oxygenated atmosphere for the body's biological needs, are essential for the self's survival.

If the developing self's normal narcissistic needs (to be elaborated upon later) are warmly accepted and empathically dealt with by those the self looks to for strength and confirmation (mother and father, for example, as the self's primary selfobjects), the developing self gradually forms firm internal psychological structures (self-cohesion). The solidness of the self is experienced as a state of general well-being. The person experiences his body as comfortable and reliable, his thoughts as perceptive and normal, his emotions as alive and manageable. This developed solidarity of the self's cohesion, reinforced by continuing empathic responses from selfobject others to the self's always present narcissistic needs, enables the individual to live a generally joyful, creative, and productive life.

The development of a healthy self-structure is the basis for our engaging life with zest, consistency, hope, and faith. A cohesive self is motivated by its own unfolding ambitions and high ideals. Such self-development, furthermore, allows a person to relate to others with deep, supportive empathy, that is, to provide that psychologically oxygenated environment for others, as others have done for the person. When, in the process of life, the cohesively formed self receives inevitable injuries to its self (called "narcissistic injuries," such as belittlement or rejection, unexpected blows to body images through disease or athletic defeat, or assaults on comfortable ideas or religious beliefs), the self is shaken, more or less, but does not become "fragmented." The disruptions to the self, while perhaps powerful, are yet transitory. The capacity and inclination to approach others with empathic understanding remain strong. Emotional boundaries stay basically intact, and thought processes do not seriously regress, even though the self may have to alter its beliefs and expectations.

Groups have a "self" analogous to the "self" of the individual. If the group's narcissistic needs are responded to by significant selfobject figures, the group develops a firm self-structure. Once reliable solidarity is established, the group's self-cohesion and self-esteem are basically sustained by its own chosen ambitions, guiding ideals, and internal encouragement. Over time, the self-assurance of the group, supported by continual affirmations of its worth and value from selfobject figures, keeps the group realistically but hopefully engaging the world. Such a healthy group-self retains its basic self-esteem when ridiculed or rejected, and continues to extend its designated support or service to others.

What are the developmental consequences, however, if the self is surrounded by a milieu of inconsistent, inadequate, or distorted selfobject responses? The answer, in brief, is that the self-structure becomes defectively weak and disordered. The self of an individual or group thereby suffers traumatic setbacks in development. Mildly to severely vulnerable individuals or groups are formed, the latter exemplified in the case of Rev. David F. and the "second-best" church. A self suffering such narcissistic difficulties as a consequence of flawed selfobject involvements remains hypersensitive to criticism, angry when not responded to as wished or willed, compelled to retaliate in some way for injuries received, and often inclined toward depression and hopelessness.

Inasmuch as the weak or defectively structured self lacks the capacity to regulate internal and external tensions, and to maintain a sense of well-being and assurance, the self still looks intensely for selfobject figures who will fulfill these functions for it. Selfobjects are expected to soothe and reassure the self of the individual or group through praise, adoration, or some other intense means of self-restoration. Without the vitalizing ministrations of the self's selfobjects, the person or group fears continued self-disintegration.

Since the self of any individual, however, is never impervious to "injuries," and since there are normal variations in our self-cohesion, all of us are vulnerable to some degree, individual and group alike. That is the normal condition of life, the human condition. All of us strive to maintain, or have restored to us, the assuredness of our self. Our efforts to ward off the hurt, embarrassment, or rage when our self-esteem is injured, the struggles to overcome our feelings of fragmentation, the yearning to experience a deep well-being of body, mind, and spirit—these stand out as major human needs of our time.

The situation and predicament of the minister is the same as that of the people whom he would serve. Psychologically, the self of the pastor is what he brings to others. I and Thou are self and self. If we believe that God works through human relationships, then the self of the pastor is the means of grace made available to others. The development and the fostering of a pastor's self, therefore, is not only a personal issue, but a vocational one as well.[1] Being a cohesive person (having a cohesive self-structure) and being a cohesive, empathic minister are intricately related. Although, thankfully, God's work through us is not limited by the quality of the human vessel, the self of the person does shape how the Word is heard and received.

While the selves of the pastor and the congregation are expressed in ministry, they are also exposed and recast in the process of ministry, for good or ill. When self of pastor and self of parish meet, there is possibility for growth, transformation, and healing, as each serves as a supportive selfobject for the other. There is also the near inevitability that some degree of tension, hurt, and anger will arise, as they fail to provide for each other the narcissistic nourishment their selves require. The wide spectrum of pastor and parish struggles are essentially grounded in momentary or long established psychological disturbances in the self-structure of each.

RESISTANCES TO SELF-INTROSPECTION

This attempt to reflect on the narcissistic needs of our individual self and community self will not be easy. Self-introspection always injures us to some degree, even when we ask for it. To a certain extent it is quite normal for us to resist recognizing and confronting our specific narcissistic needs, our own, or our group's. As pastors, for example, it is embarrassing for us to admit our self's need for being "mirrored," or for "merging" with "idealized" figures, or for immersing ourself with others whom we consider our "alterego" (the three central narcissistic needs of the self).

These terms may hold little threat until we realize how they are sometimes expressed in our lives: Our secret wishes for fame, our longing to be seen as special, our efforts to stand out in admired, applauded ways, our inner expectation that our body, mind, family, and congregation will respond to our guiding control (our need to be mirrored; Rev. David F.'s central narcissistic need-demand); our tender yearnings to be physically touched, smiled graciously upon, or made to be part of the lives of persons whose being reassures and empowers us (expressions of our need to merge with idealized figures); our disguised efforts to pay only minimal, dutiful attention to those who are different from us, and to relate primarily, if not exclusively, with others we deem as "just like me" (our need for alterego relating).

In essence, these narcissistic needs are normal, just as our needs for love are normal. When these needs for being mirrored, for merging with idealized individuals, and for alterego relating are adequately met by empathically responding selfobject others, we feel whole inside, cohesive. We embrace life with hope and our duties with confident zest. If, however, such needs are thwarted time and again, we are filled with emptiness, and vulnerable sensitivities give way to vaulting rage and/or plunge into pits of despair.

It is painful, furthermore, for us ministers to recall: the humiliation when we have felt slighted in public or ignored by our congregations (injuries to our mirroring efforts); the emotional devastation when we have presented ourselves in some fashion to persons we admired and then felt brushed aside or patronized by them (an injury to our idealizing need); or the aching sense of not being "normal," and not "belonging," when others fail to convey in some manner that their thoughts, feelings, and motivations are like our own thoughts, feelings, and motivations (an injury to our alterego yearnings). We try to hide or rationalize away our responses of rage, which long for retaliation against those who have acted insensitively toward us. We try to hide or rationalize our responses of withdrawal, where in our private inner world we nurse our wounds by wrapping our selves in the balm of self-pity. The resistances of a pastor to opening himself to personal or professional narcissistic longings is nothing more than the fear of being traumatically injured again. In one sense, then, resistance aims at survival of the self. On the other hand, however, resistance militates against the transformation of distorted, archaic narcissistic needs, leading eventually to increased hypersensitivity, fragmentation, and destructive behavior. These dynamics apply as well to the group self of a congregation.

A pastor or parish's resistance to self-reflection becomes stronger, even demonic, when their self-esteem (self-cohesion) is perpetually fragile and easily injured, and when, feeling their very survival is at stake, they establish highly justified measures for dealing with those who have or will dare become a threat to their particular beliefs, rituals, or policies. The pristine congregation, who in consistory meetings reminded their associate pastor that she was "just a hired hand here," and the imperious pastor, who regularly resigned from his congregation as a means of controlling polity and program, are both unlikely to be open to any suggestion that beneath it all they struggle with serious disturbances in the structure and coherence of their group and individual selves; in short, with narcissistic difficulties.

Narcissistic needs are a normal part of us. We do not

outgrow them, although they unfold into higher forms, and we mature in how we need to have them met. How the narcissistic needs of a person are responded to by others determines how the person's self is formed. Healthy responses from others to these narcissistic needs eventually result in the development of a healthy self. Adequate self-development is evident, in part, in persons who are assured of their cohesiveness through time, firm in their sense of worth, and joyfully alive in spirit and emotion. Inadequate or overly intense responses from others to the self and its narcissistic needs, however, result in persons whose sense of self-cohesion is uncertain and fragile, whose self-esteem is vulnerable and easily injured, and whose zest in living is minimal or lacking.

Self psychology illuminates the presence and power of narcissistic strivings in the self of the individual and in the group self of corporate entities, and provides insight into the development of healthy or weak selves via the nature of responses to the self's narcissistic needs. The "self" and its nuclear requirements for life's well-being deserve to be redeemed by the larger church, just as more recently the centrality of our body and of our sexuality for understanding and living out our religious faith has become theologically embraced.[2]

Historically, however, such "narcissistic" feelings and actions have been declared "sinful." The psychological disavowal by pastors and congregations of even normal narcissistic strivings is buttressed by traditional theological injunctions against all but a few narcissistic inclinations. A person of God eschews prideful yearnings, turns the other cheek when belittled, empties self in forgiving service to *all* others, those like him as well as those acutely dissimilar, and finds true self in the process of losing it. Within the range of narcissistic motives, only an effort such as merging with God as the omnipotent, idealized figure is deemed appropriate. On the whole, narcissistic strivings and the authentic Christian life have been pronounced antithetical. Yet the self's narcissistic strivings are part of us, in all their created goodness, as well as in their defective grossness.

The term and concept of "self" dealt with here is of the highest order. In no way does it imply self-centeredness, nor does the full development of the "self" lead to forms of cultural narcissism, to what has popularly been tagged as the "me-generation." Various religious commentators, along with social critics, have denounced any psychology that supports persons turning inward upon self-need, rather than outward toward responsible caring for others. There is justification in these criticisms. But it overshoots the mark to say that *any* psychological perspective that focuses on the needs and centrality of the self "is part of the problem of modern life rather than part of its resolution."[3] In what follows, therefore, we will be interpreting the struggles of pastors and parishes from a sensitive understanding of the self's centrality in our individual and corporate life.

Chapter 2

A WORKING OVERVIEW OF THE SELF PSYCHOLOGY PERSPECTIVE

Self psychology has both an individual "self" and a group "self." The group self is self psychology as an enduring, developing psychological approach that advances: a theory of self-development; a description-diagnosis of healthy and pathological narcissistic manifestations in persons and in groups; a mode of treatment for individuals suffering from disorders of the self; and a broad therapeutic orientation for restoration of our Western culture. While originating from the insights of Heinz Kohut, self psychology now has, based upon Kohut's seminal work, a group life of its own. Colleagues and collaborators have produced several edited volumes of essays on self psychology, exploring and expanding its perspective. The most prominent of these are: *The Psychology of the Self: A Casebook* (1978); *Advances in Self Psychology* (1980); *The Future of Psychoanalysis* (1983); *Empathy I* and *Empathy II* (1984); *Self Psychology and the Humanities* (1985); *Progress in Self Psychology,* Vol. I (1985); and *Progress in Self Psychology,* Vol. 2 (1986).

As Arnold Goldberg, the editor of the first three and the last two volumes, intimates, self psychology has achieved a momentum and a "history" of its own.[1] The individual self of self psychology is, of course, the person of Kohut. At this point in its history, self psychology owes much of its character and body of insights to this man. Inasmuch as the elaboration and application of self psychology to the narcissistic struggles of pastors and parishes is based principally upon Kohut's insights, a brief opening word about him is in order.

THE SELF OF HEINZ KOHUT

Heinz Kohut was born into an upper middle class family in the old world of Vienna on May 3, 1913. He was an only child. According to him, loneliness was a shaping factor in his life. His father was in the army for 4 years, serving on the Russian front during all of World War I. Kohut and his mother lived with her parents until Kohut was five. During this time he become emotionally attached to his maternal grandfather, who died before Kohut's father returned. Later, Kohut spent his boyhood summers and budding adolescence in Swiss and French boarding schools away from home. There he would receive postcards from his mother at one end of Europe and from his father at the other. What "saved" him, as he said, were the museums, concert halls, and books. These were his world, his home, and his friends. His own artistic talent showed itself early in a literary form. He wrote poetry, and at the age of twelve produced the libretto for an opera.

In the 1930s, while working on a medical degree, he became interested in psychoanalysis. He entered analysis with August Eichorn, who was a close friend of Freud's. Although Kohut's time in Vienna overlapped that of Freud's, Kohut saw the founder of psychoanalysis only once, that being in 1938 when he tipped his hat to the elderly man as Freud sat alone in a railroad coach awaiting his enforced exile from Austria. According to Kohut's fond telling, Freud tipped his hat in return as the train pulled out.

In 1939, after receiving his medical degree from the University of Vienna, Kohut followed Freud's path to Great Britain. One year later he sailed for the United States, cutting back and forth across the Atlantic to avoid submarines and mine fields. He arrived with barely a quarter in his pocket. He soon settled in Chicago where he learned English rapidly and fluently, and explored the city that would become his home for the next 40 years. He applied for residency in neurology at the University of Chicago where he was accepted and where he remained on the faculty for many years. He impressed everyone he met. It is said that neurologists at the University still talk of the loss to their field when Kohut left for an assistant professorship in neurology and psychiatry in 1944, and then only in psychiatry in 1947.[2] When he graduated from the Institute for Psychoanalysis in 1948, he was immediately brought onto the faculty and staff. Once established there, he never left. He became an renowned teacher and a brilliant analyst to whom seasoned psychoanalysts came for consultation on their own cases.

Kohut also provided distinguished leadership for the psychoanalytic community at large. He served as president of the American Psychoanalytic Association, and was former vice president of the International Psychoanalytic Association. During this time he was an eminent spokesman for classical Freudian thought, and widely respected by Anna Freud, Heinz Hartmann, and others.

Kohut's first book, *The Analysis of the Self* (1971), signaled a sharp departure from the tradition of classical psychoanalysis, however. It represented an evolutionary stage not only in Kohut's thinking but in the development of psychoanalysis itself. This work, along with *The Restoration of the Self* (1977), illuminates the new understandings and far-ranging implications emerging from Kohut's work with narcissistically disturbed persons. His many invaluable contributions to psychoanalytic theory and concepts have been gathered in a two-volume work entitled, *The Search for the Self*.

In October 1981, after a courageous struggle with what had become the weakness of his body, Heinz Kohut died. There was never, however, even at the end, a weariness of his mind. In the very midst of his dying he wrote his final contribution to depth psychology, indeed, to humankind, published posthumously under the title: *How Does Analysis Cure?* (1984).

A few months before he died, I had the very good fortune to meet with Heinz Kohut in his home near the University of Chicago. He had been intrigued by my article, "Soteriological Dimensions in the Work of Heinz Kohut",[3] which caused him, he said, to scurry to the dictionary for clarification of the first word. Graciously and promptly he agreed to meet to discuss what I had purposed, namely his understanding of religion from the self psychology framework. In our first session it became clear that Kohut was opposed to a methodology that merely "applied" the self psychology perspective to the nonanalytic material of religion. Religion and depth psychology, particularly self psychology, needed to develop a reciprocal relationship, he stressed. Each had much to learn from the other.

Later, at the memorial service for Dr. Kohut held at the First Unitarian Church in Chicago where he was a member, I was suddenly struck by the implications of our meetings. Charles Kligerman, a close friend and colleague of Kohut's, stated in that service that during the last 2 years of his life, Kohut held body and soul together by sheer willpower alone. With all that was pressing from within and from without at that time, it seems highly significant to me that Kohut would have spent a portion of his precious final days talking to a clergyman-psychologist about religion and self psychology. This was, perhaps, more than a normal continuation of expanding his framework to other areas of human endeavor. It was also a powerful indication of the value and importance Kohut placed upon religion for the maintenance, support, and uplifting of persons—in the midst of life, as well as at its end.

I relate this for two primary reasons. First, self psychology, as Kohut perceived it, is not opposed to our religious or spiritual life, nor to our communities of faith. His meetings with me openly revealed the value he placed on religion. Second, although within these pages we are utilizing the self psychology framework to illuminate the pattern and character of pastor-parish struggles, Kohut affirms the necessity for reciprocal enrichment. Religion, he emphasized, has much to teach depth psychology.

While Kohut's death deprived us of his further creative unfoldings, the impact of his new scientific paradigm will continue richly to bless the study and the care of the self. The foundation for this perpetuation rests in large measure upon the clinical and cultural value of Kohut's insights into the nature of selfhood. Kohut's work offers deepened appreciations and new understandings into the character of our self, and of our plight in this modern Western world. His view of the self as moving toward creative expression of its inner life, as struggling to live on the basis of higher values and meanings where encompassing empathy for self and for others is paramount, this provides the basis for hope, hope that warrants and enables committed effort, although it cannot justify sanguine optimism.

Furthermore, interpretations of selfhood can make important differences in how women and men live their lives. Psychological theories, as well as religious doctrines, have the power to elevate or degrade an individual's sense of self and his interactions with others. Kohut's clinical perspective on the nature of the self involved him simultaneously in a moral battle against debilitating assumptions about personhood associated with certain features of depth psychology and with certain forms of religious belief. Kohut's self psychology, therefore, contributes to the enhancement of human life through a transformation, as well as a buttressing, of our religious and psychological thoughts about our selves.

CLINICAL FOUNDATIONS OF SELF PSYCHOLOGY

In order for us to proceed, the reader is not obliged to have a comprehensive grasp of the whole scope of self psychology, nor to agree with all the dimensions of its framework. In essence, in this chapter I will lift out the three narcissistic needs of the self (and the required nature of the responses to these needs by "selfobject" others) that Kohut discusses as essential for the healthy development of our self. They are: mirroring needs/responses, idealizing needs/responses, alterego needs/responses. Utilizing these, I will describe and interpret the narcissistic disturbances in the lives of pastors (Chapter 3) and in the lives of parishes (Chapter 4), and then indicate how a pastor's particular, dominant narcissistic need meeting a congregations's particular, dominant narcissistic need creates various patterns of interaction and struggle (Chapter 5). The reader, however, should have some appreciation of the power of these conceptual observations specifically, which entails, therefore, some general appreciation of the unique focus of self psychology, to which we now turn.

Kohut's self psychology insights developed out of his many years of psychoanalytic work with patients in analysis with him. Some of these patients were struggling with problems of conflicting libidinal (sexual) drives, which the psychological literature called, in general, "the neuroses."

For these psychosexual conflictual difficulties, the traditional psychoanalytic approach, which centered principally around oedipal issues, was considered the appropriate treatment method. But Kohut also worked with another type of patient, which the psychological literature called, in general, "narcissistic." This patient was characterized by a specific vulnerability: his self-esteem was unusually unstable and, in particular, he was extremely sensitive to failures, disappointments, and slights.

Therapists in the past, of course, had observed these narcissistic characteristics in patients they treated. Classical psychoanalysis (that branch of psychoanalysis that accepted and closely followed Sigmund Freud's analytic formulations and approaches) considered narcissistic individuals as characterologically fixated at a primitive phase in psychosexual development, referred to as the "autoerotic stage."

Very broadly stated, the individual was considered self-absorbed, involved more with self-love than with love for others. Mature psychic development meant, for traditional psychoanalysis, that an individual would eventually pass through and basically relinquish this early narcissistic (autoerotic, self-love) stage in the process of forming solid "object relationships," where persons would be experienced and related to as objects separate from the individual's self, and where, in the forming of "object love" ties, the individual would be characterized more by emotional investment in others than in self.

Mature object relation ties were considered the result of healthy psychosexual development. Narcissistic, autoerotic preoccupations were considered the result of thwarted or delayed psychosexual development. Classical psychoanalysis, therefore, tended to interpret all personality and behavior disorders as representing some aspect of psychosexual conflict, whether at an early stage of sexual development or late. Furthermore, traditional psychoanalysis believed that narcissistically bound individuals could not be treated by psychoanalysis since, being so focused on themselves (in the autoerotic, self-love stage), and not sufficiently able to experience others as separate persons (not able to form object relationships), they were unable to form a transference relationship to the therapist that was the prime means for analytic cure.

As Kohut worked with "narcissistic" individuals, however, the formulations of classical psychoanalysis did not seem to fit what he was experiencing. In the first place, Kohut found that these persons *could* and *did* form a particular type of relationship to him in the therapy setting. A narcissistic patient (to whom Kohut later referred as suffering from a "narcissistic personality disorder," or "disorder of the self") would emotionally respond to Kohut as if Kohut were inseparable from the individual's very self. The patient made Kohut a psychological extension of his own inner world, where Kohut was expected to function in ways the self needed and at times demanded. Kohut felt himself no longer engaged as a person in his own right (object relations), but as one whose existence now was to be responsive, indeed, perfectly responsive, to the self of the individual. As Kohut came to name it, he had become the person's "selfobject," an object only insofar as he was connected to the person's self.

Gradually, Kohut realized that the person's self was very vulnerable. The inner psychological structure of the self showed a lack of coherence, firm self-esteem, and functional harmony. Because the person suffered from inadequate psychological structures necessary basically to sustain his own mental, emotional, and physical equilibrium, the person needed Kohut to respond to him in reassuring, affirming, and soothing ways. The vulnerable, easily upset self needed/demanded either "mirroring," "idealizing," or "alterego" selfobject responses, as Kohut eventually understood and named the particular types of relationships (transferences) the person eventually established with him.

Generally stated, Kohut's selfobject responses provided those essential life-sustaining and regulating psychological functions which the person did not have, or had only in a weak or distorted form. More particularly, only when Kohut mirrored the ideas, achievements, and actions of a mirror-hungry patient (showed empathic admiration, for example) could the person experience renewed self-esteem and regained zest for work, family, or friends. Only when Kohut allowed himself to be idealized, and to respond in ways that allowed an idealization-hungry patient to feel part of Kohut's idealized greatness and wisdom, could the person experience some degree of inner security and calmness. Only when Kohut responded to the patient's need for him to serve as a selfobject alterego (a psychological "twin" of the person), could the person be assured of being normal, of belonging, and of having an inner consistency of being through time and changing circumstances.

The narcissistically disturbed individuals could not themselves fulfill this need for the validation of their existence and the confirming of their worthwhileness. Consequently, they sought that confirmation and consolidation of their selves through the psychological presence and being of another, namely Kohut, as an available, empathic selfobject. These individuals were unconsciously transferring to him the functional responsibility for shoring up and maintaining the cohesiveness of their selves.

Kohut's patients were not psychotic. They did not generally hallucinate or lose touch with reality. They knew Kohut was a real person, that his education was different from theirs, that he had his own family of which they were not members. Nonetheless, the essential psychological nature of the human relationship was the appropriation and experience of Kohut as their selfobject. As long as Kohut fulfilled his selfobject role adequately, they felt strong and inwardly assured of their selves. When he failed in some way to be that intensely empathic selfobject responder, however, they felt empty, joyless, and responded with varying degrees of despondency and rage.

Kohut began to realize that this ebb and flow in his patients' self-esteem and self-cohesion, as Kohut either adequately fulfilled his particular selfobject roles or failed in them, were redramatizations of traumatic selfobject responses from the patients' past. Narcissistic injuries (injuries to the self) and persistent narcissistic needs not met by unresponsive or unavailable parental selfobjects were played out with Kohut and others again and again. In contrast to classical psychoanalytic thought, Kohut observed that narcissistic individuals not only could form transference relationships, but that the transference relationships also reflected, as in the neuroses, particular psychic traumas from the individuals' developmental past.

How, then, did one interpret what was happening with these narcissistic individuals? Did the perspective of traditional analysis, which held that the person was fixated at a primitive stage of psychosexual development, seem to fit? Even when narcissistically disordered individuals exhibited excessive or perverse sexual behavior and impulses, were these signs of a basic underlying difficulty in psychosexual development? In the face of all that he had been taught as a psychoanalyst, Kohut said no. Excessive or perverse sexual activities of a person with self difficulties were symptomatic indications that the person was "fragmenting," that is, the person's inner self, the psychological core and structure of the person's being, was "falling apart," with the sexual drives emerging as isolated, unintegrated impulses from an disintegrating self. Sexual drives could not be "tamed," or controlled, or channeled into productive energy because a cohesive, regulating-functioning self was absent or inadequately functioning.

This was a major reinterpretation in psychology and

psychoanalysis, not only about the nature of sexual drives and impulses, but also about the central disturbance in many psychologically struggling individuals. Yes, there are individuals whose problems are psychosexual in nature, where object relationships are formed with others, and where certain types of conflicts arise within the person, and between the person and object others, based upon unresolved psychosexual needs and anxieties. But there is also a separate line of difficulties, where problems with *self* rather than *sex* are central, where selfobject relationships characterize the person's way of incorporating the world, and where problems within the individual and with others revolve around unfulfilled narcissistic needs and inadequately structured selves.

Kohut observed and then articulated a perspective in which the developmental history and drama of the self's unfolding was as crucial in personality formation as the history of psychosexual development. More significantly, he observed and then articulated an approach in which the vulnerable and cohesion-lacking self could be strengthened in therapy when the person's narcissistic needs and history of selfobject traumas were empathically considered. Whereas, formerly, such individuals were considered beyond the reach of psychological care and cure, Kohut's new psychoanalytic understandings led to new possibilities for the restoration of suffering selves.

NARCISSISTIC NEEDS AND TRANSFERENCES

From years of psychoanalytic work with narcissistically disturbed individuals, Kohut became ever more cognizant of mirroring and idealizing narcissistic needs as they appeared repeatedly in the selfobject transferences that his patients established with him. In the "mirroring transference," the person expected to be admired and applauded for whatever he brought to Kohut. These expectations ranged from blatant elicitations to hesitating, veiled longings. If, in the therapy relationship, Kohut was emphatically receptive to the person's intellectual or physical achievements, or to his subtle or grandiose declarations of "being better than others," the individual felt inwardly firm and outwardly invigorated. The narcissistic need here was for "mirroring." The individual psychologically required consistent and near-perfect mirroring responses in order to ward off intense feelings of emptiness and vulnerability, to maintain and restore self-esteem, and to preserve some semblance of self-cohesion.

Other persons formed a different narcissistic transference to Kohut, an "idealizing" transference. (In actuality, Kohut's patients often demonstrated both types of narcissistic selfobject needs, although one typically dominated.) In this transference configuration, if Kohut allowed the person to admire him, to idealize him, and if Kohut as the idealized selfobject responded empathically to the person's wish to merge with Kohut's greatness or be soothed by Kohut's calming power, the person's inner turmoil was quieted, and daily existence felt more manageable, if not hopeful. The person felt "put back on my feet again."

Later, in his unfolding discoveries concerning our narcissistic requirements, Kohut recognized a third major narcissistic need: the need for "alterego" selfobject responses. The transference to Kohut in this case was not the wish to merge with him as the idealized selfobject, nor to have him as the mirroring selfobject admire the grandiose self's presentations; instead, the person yearned to experience Kohut as being essentially the same as the person's own self—indeed, to experience Kohut as a psychological twin. If Kohut empathically responded to the person's need for appropriating him as an alterego in thought, feeling, belief, judgment, and other essential characteristics, the person experienced a sense of being an included part of the human family, of being normal and belonging to others like-minded and like-spirited, and of having an inner, consistent core of qualities, skills, and attributes that could be relied upon to remain over time and in changing circumstances.[4]

Kohut's empathic selfobject responses to an individual's need for mirroring, or idealizing, or alterego in-tuneness, resulted in a diminution of the person's intense disintegration anxiety and vulnerability, and a rise in feelings of intactness, well-being, and self-assurance. Clinically stated, at those moments, the self had regained, or established, some semblance of self-cohesion: which, however, was extremely unreliable. The person lacked those essential psychological structures that make for internal firmness of the personality and that, through their functions, maintain and restore self-cohesion when the self is injured in some way. Those capacities of the self to sustain its self-esteem when ignored or humiliated, for example, were defective, distorted, or weak. The person, therefore, relied upon constantly available mirroring selfobject responses to provide some degree of internal firmness via a buttressing of the person's self-esteem.

The narcissistically vulnerable individual, therefore, was hypersensitive to any semblance of rejection or ridicule, and needed the presence of continuous and near-perfect selfobject responses in order to experience an assuredness of physical, emotional, and mental well-being. The selfobject need/demand of course outstripped all possibilities for fulfillment. Inevitably, the narcissistically disturbed individual experienced Kohut as flawed and failing. When this happened, the person was crestfallen, depleted. A wide spectrum of rageful reactions also poured out at the one who had dared to be so insensitive.

NORMAL AND PATHOLOGICAL NARCISSISTIC DEVELOPMENT

Kohut's work focused on these dynamics: the recurring patterns of need for mirroring, idealizing, and alterego selfobject responses; the inevitable narcissistic injuries suffered by the self when selfobject responses were unavailable or inadequate; the consequent "fragmentation" (disintegration) of the self; the rise of depressive withdrawal or narcissistic rage; and the bit-by-bit process of regaining some semblance of self-cohesion. From ongoing analysis, Kohut came to realize that the persistent selfobject needs and the hypersensitivity to being slighted were revivals—reenactments in the therapy—of unfulfilled selfobject needs and actual traumatic injuries to the self from unempathic, parental selfobjects occurring during early developmental years. From this clinical base Kohut also formulated that *the narcissistic needs of the self are normal, healthy developmental needs,* and not symptoms of pathological fixation or regression, as suggested by traditional psychoanalysis.

Moreover, Kohut stressed that *the psychologically oxygenated milieu of selfobject responses to the narcissistic requirements of the self constituted the very foundation of all psychological life.* Self psychology, therefore, is invested in examining, identifying, and defining the health-enhancing factors in individual and group life, as well as examining those factors that produce disordered individual and group selves. The following captions and brief descriptions provide a summary of Kohut's understanding of the self's healthy and pathological narcissistic development.[5]

The Primary Psychological Configuration.   From early on, the child expresses normal needs to be watched, enjoyed, encouraged. To all of its actions and antics, physical and verbal, the child needs admiring, applauding responses from empathic others, responses that vitalize and affirm/confirm the very being of the child in all its physical-emotional-mental wholeness. At the same time, the child expresses normal needs to be soothed, to be reassured when frightened, and to be emotionally uplifted when he falters or fails. The child needs to be embraced by powerful others into whose strength and calmness he can merge for comfort when injured in some way.

The child requires, furthermore, empathic involvements from others that assure him that he belongs, that his skill and talents, movements and efforts, are reflected in the lives of similar others. Being surrounded by others the child experiences as "the same as me" gives the child a sense of being "normal," anchors the child's self-continuity, and provides the sustaining power of knowing one belongs, to particular groups and to the human family.

The aspect of the self that calls for "mirroring" of its grandly paraded activity is the "grandiose-mirroring self." The aspect of the self that looks for "merger" with idealized, omnipotent others is the "idealizing-merger self." The aspect of the self that seeks "twinship" relationships is the "alterego self." Those from whom the self expects mirroring, idealizing, alterego responses are the self's "selfobjects."

The nuclear self of the child (its narcissistic needs and quality of self-cohesion) and the world of its selfobjects together form the bedrock of all psychological life. *The primary psychological experience, from which all other aspects of development are based, is the "self-selfobject" experience, that relationship between the self and its more or less empathic selfobjects.* Here it is that the filling in, firming up, and consolidation of the self occurs. Here it is that the experience of the absence, weakness, or distortion of the life-sustaining empathic responsiveness of others threatens the very core and organization of the self, leading to varying degrees of disintegration anxiety, and leaving the injured self (child) with a chronic struggle to maintain physical, emotional, mental, and spiritual equilibrium the best it can.

Optimal Conditions.   Optimal conditions for development occur when the parents, as the primary selfobjects, adequately fulfill the selfobject role in two ways. First, they are willing and able to mirror, be idealized, or alterego the child's archaic narcissistic wishes. Second, and at the same time, they are willing and able to provide "optimal frustrations" of these wishes, which are the inevitable disappointments to the child that the parent allows and even makes necessary; always, however, with continued support for the child who will experience some degree of deflation and/or rage. When these optimal selfobject responses are made, there is the gradual transformation of the child's archaically expressed narcissistic needs into internal, stable psychological self-structure (a cohesive nuclear self is being formed).

Normal Development.   In the optimally frustrating, empathic environment provided by the parental selfobjects, the child's archaic grandiose self gradually becomes transformed into mature forms of grandiosity. Here the self is motivated and supported by its mature ambitions and purposes, and is able to regulate and reliably maintain its own self-esteem. The nuclear self "transmutes" the experiences with adequate mirroring selfobjects into its own internal structure, fulfilling the functions that once were normally and necessarily served by the archaic mirroring selfobjects. The self's own ambitions and purposes, hopefully and energetically carried out, are the transformed essence of early mirroring selfobject responses to the archaic grandiose self. While still relying upon selfobject mirroring of its grandiose self throughout life, the self becomes increasingly able to maintain much of its own self-esteem when injured in some way, is less prone to "fragmentation," and no longer requires archaic selfobject responses to abate the episodic loss of self-cohesion.

The idealizing self becomes transformed into mature forms of idealization, where the self is able to calm, comfort, and compose its self and to be guided by the leadership and inspiration of its ideals and values. As with the grandiose self, idealized selfobject responses are "transmuted," i.e., become part and parcel of the psychic structure of the self. The self's ideals and values that uplift the self, and the self's capacity for self-soothing and reassurance, are the transformed psychic essence of the self's early experiences with empathically responding idealized selfobjects. While still relying upon the availability of idealized selfobjects throughout life, the self relies more upon the memory of empathic resonance with idealized others; upon the knowledge that one shares the visions and values of admired individuals never met; and upon the uplifting awareness that one's life is immersed in and dedicated to ideals of great meaning and importance.

Similarly, the archaic alterego "twinship" needs of the self become transmuted into mature alterego inclinations (i.e., inclinations to seek out others who reflect and reinforce the essential qualities of the self), and into the self's internal, firm assurance of being normal and of belonging. The sense of being normal in thought, word, feeling, and deed, and the comforting assurance that one fits in and belongs, to particular groups of kindred souls and to the human family at large, are the transformed psychic essence of empathic echoes to the self's alterego longings. Firm assurance of alterego connections sustains a self when the self is isolated, confined, or its identity threatened, inasmuch as the self experiences being surrounded by silent, invisible others who, as kindred spirits, resonate with the self's very being.

Faulty Conditions.   If, however, there are massive shortcomings in maternal and paternal selfobject responses, and the optimal frustration conditions are not met, then defects, distortions, and weaknesses in the structure of the self occur.

Abnormal Development.   The archaic grandiose aspect of the self may persist into adult life, basically unaltered or inadequately altered. Those direct, consistent, and perfect mirroring responses expected by the child's grandiose self, normal and appropriate for the child's phase of development, are carried into adulthood, basically unmodified, without being transformed into healthy self-structure and into healthy expressions of the self's grandiosity. The narcissistically disordered self will still look for archaic mirroring responses to his physical attributes, sexual suaveness, mental superiority, or financial success, for example. The unmodified or inadequately modified grandiose self becomes the dominant, psychologically organizing principle of the individual's life.

Similarly, the archaic idealizing aspect of the self may persist, basically unaltered or inadequately altered. Here the self will continue to search for omnipotent (idealized) figures with which to merge ideologically, financially, emotionally, or physically. The unmodified idealization need becomes the cardinal, psychologically organizing principle in the person's life. Or archaic alterego twinship needs may persist into adulthood, with the person rigidly demanding that others feel, think, and act in the same way he does. This, too, may become the central organizing principle of the person's psychological existence, determining, by its intensity, the very survival of the individual.

Pathology and Symptomatology.   Narcissistically disturbed individuals are suffering from an insufficient consolidation of the self (self-cohesion). Manifestations are: vulnerable self-esteem; feelings of emptiness, joylessness, meaninglessness; lack of initiative and/or hyperexcitability; a variety of sexual, perverse activities; a diffused sensitivity to peo-

ple; hypochondriasis. These arise because the person lacks
the development of solid, internal self-structures needed
to: regulate self-esteem when injured; infuse personal goals
and ideals with energy and hope; utilize what selfobject
support is offered; and channel the impulses and drives
of the body.

The person's narcissistic equilibrium is extremely vulnerable. To real or imagined slights, he responds with
shamefaced withdrawal and depression, or with "narcissistic
rage." The process of losing self-cohesion is called "fragmentation." Fragmentation refers to a spectrum of experiences, all of which point to the feeling and state of losing
hold of one's self. Bodily, it can range from the schizoid
reaction that one's arm is not one's own, to upset stomachs,
tight chests, and heart palpitations in anxious situations.
Emotionally, it can range from the borderline reaction
where one feels one is "withering away" or "disappearing,"
to the more common experience expressed as, "I feel like
I'm falling apart and can't pull myself together." Mentally
it can range from full-blown paranoid delusions to the
confused, listless thinking of one who is depressed. A narcissistically vulnerable individual will involve himself in
numerous activities, mature to archaic, to counteract this
frightening fragmentation of his nuclear self.

THE SPECTRUM OF MIRRORING, IDEALIZATION, AND ALTER-EGO NEEDS

Kohut did not believe that mirroring, idealization, and
alterego needs exhausted the type and range of the self's
narcissistic requirements from infancy to old age. These
three, however, he considered essentially central to the
survival and well-being of the self of individuals. A decisive
body of psychological literature has developed supporting
the formative influence of selfobject responses to these el-

Table 2-1 Grandiose-Mirroring Needs
The need of the self to experience selfobjects mirroring its own grandiosity

Spectrum of Grandiose-Mirroring Needs	
Archaic Mirroring Needs	*Mature Mirroring Needs*
(Normal requirements of early life, but: (1) chronically present in disorders of the self; (2) passingly present in periods of special stress in those free from self pathology)	(Selfobject requirements we all need for psychological survival from birth to death)
Some persons manifest a need for direct, constant, and near perfect admiration and enthusiasm for their actions, words, thoughts, and creations. Others are experienced and appropriated as merely extensions of the persons' archaic grandiose selves. Constant attentiveness (mirroring) by selfobject others is needed, inasmuch as the persons are not internally able to maintain or regulate their own self-esteem or be sustained by their own projects and goals. Without selfobjects serving these psychological functions via their empathic mirroring role, the persons are in danger of further collapse of their self-cohesion. Great rage arises when selfobjects fail to be empathically responsive. Despondence and deep self-doubts also emerge.	All persons have the need to experience the pride and increased sense of well-being when their thought, work, and being is applauded by others. Such mirroring responses help persons maintain healthy feelings of self-esteem, contribute to the pleasurable pursuit of goals, and lead persons to be empathically supportive of others' mirroring needs. The memory of being special, coupled with reassurances in the present, is the basis by which persons are able to maintain their self-worth and energetically continue with their efforts even when others are unresponsive or outright critical.

Table 2-2   Idealization-Merger Needs
The need of the self to experience merger with idealized selfobjects

Spectrum of Idealization-Merger Needs	
Archaic Idealization Needs	*Mature Idealization Needs*
(Normal requirements of early life, but: (1) chronically present in disorders of the self; (2) passingly present in periods of special stress in those free of self pathology)	(Selfobject requirements we all need for psychological survival from birth to death)
Some persons manifest a constant and direct need to be connected with and made to feel part of individuals they deem omnipotent (selfobject) figures. Inasmuch as these persons lack the internal psychological capacity to soothe and uplift their selves, they seek to merge with calming, empowering idealized figures. These persons express great sensitivity to being rejected and slighted, and are markedly vigilant for signs that the idealized one is failing to fulfill the idealized role. When the person does sense rejection or becomes disillusioned with the heroic figure, intense rage may ensue, with the wish (attempt) to do away with the one who has so utterly disappointed the person. Depletion, lifelessness, and deep self-doubts also emerge.	All persons have the need to feel part of admired individuals whose lives, deeds, and ideals they can embrace and make their own. The capacity of persons to be uplifted by values and ideals transmitted by inspiring others—that persons incorporate and feel in partnership with—contributes to their sense of inner security and calmness, and moves them to care for others with the same uplifting spirit they have experienced. The sense of merger with idealized figures and with sustaining values and ideals helps us maintain hope when threats to the meaning and purpose of our life and the lives of others storm in upon us.

Table 2-3   Alterego Needs
The need of the self to experience selfobjects as its alterego

Spectrum of Alterego Needs	
Archaic Alterego Needs	*Mature Alterego Needs*
(Normal requirements of early life, but: (1) chronically present in disorders of the self; (2) passingly present in periods of special stress in those free of self pathology)	(Selfobject requirements we all need for psychological survival from birth to death)
Some persons exhibit a constant need to experience others as being identical with their selves in all essential ways. These persons search for involvements with others who are like their selves, often feeling (and reacting to) others as the persons' "twin." Intense (selfobject) alterego responses are needed in order for the persons to feel human and normal in body, mind, and emotion, to sense securely that they "belong," and to confirm an inner constancy of being. Panic arises when these persons feel alone or are not surrounded by others "just like me." Rage also arises when expected alteregos fail to function as available, empathic "twins."	All persons have the need to experience a sense of unity with others perceived as like unto their selves. Relationships with kindred spirits affirm their own unique humanness, enhance the enjoyment of shared activities, and provide an assuredness of belonging and togetherness through all the struggles of life. The abiding sense that there are others "like me" can sustain a person when, by force or other circumstances, the person is placed in a foreign environment that threatens his personal and social identity.

emental narcissistic needs of the individual (and to the narcissistic needs of groups, as we shall discuss).[6] Mirroring, idealizing, and alterego needs exist along a spectrum, from archaic, unmodified narcissistic forms in the individual (or group), through to higher order, transformed narcissistic expressions in the lives of persons (and groups).

Inasmuch as I contend that the struggles of pastors and parishes, and the struggles between pastors and parishes, often reflect the presence and persistence of archaic narcissistic needs in each, I have summarized in diagrammatic form the nature and spectrum of these three configurations of narcissistic need. It is important to accent here that selfobject figures used for the creation and sustenance of the self also undergo lifelong maturation and development. Kohut makes it clear that we must not confuse (1) archaic selfobjects that (a) are the normal requirements of early life, and (b) are required later on in a chronic way by a person suffering a self disorder, with (2) the mature selfobjects that all of us need for our psychological survival from birth to death.

NEW PERSPECTIVES IN SELF PSYCHOLOGY

From this clinical work with narcissistically disturbed individuals evolved significant advances in the way of understanding, dealing with, and helping the self of the individual (and the self of a group). As indicated, a significant psychological advance has been made in the diagnosis and treatment of persons suffering from disorders of the self. Kohut's work brings narcissistically disturbed individuals within the boundary of human, scientific care giving, where they, as well as their symptoms, are met with broad empathic understanding.

Along with this comes a major advance in the theory of psychological development. Traditional psychoanalytic theory claims that narcissism is a primary psychological state into which the child is born but out of which he eventually develops. In normal development, it is held, primary narcissism becomes healthy object love, that is, love of others as individuals separate from the self. Selfobject relating, therefore, is a fixation at or a regression to a primitive state, and a clear sign of pathology.

From painstaking examination of his own clinical data, however, and from clinical collaboration with colleagues, Kohut and self psychology came to understand that narcissism (self-selfobject relating) develops *without* changing over into object love. Kohut deduced that there are normally two lines of psychic development: one for object love and one for narcissism. Narcissism, consequently, should be seen as a *normal, separate line of psychological development.*

Furthermore, just as object love (love of others as separate objects) develops from archaic states to mature states, so also does the line of narcissism develop from archaic states to mature states. Narcissism has mature forms as well as primitive and pathological forms. In an article now famous in self psychology circles, Kohut demonstrates how those characteristics of human life so prized—empathy, humor, wisdom, creativity, and cosmic consciousness, for example—are expressions of narcissism in its highest form.[7] The roots of these human achievements are grounded in the separate line of narcissistic development.

Self psychology affirms in particular, therefore, that we should learn to acknowledge as normal and legitimate our narcissistic strivings to shine, be admired, or feel indispensable (expressions of our self's grandiosity-mirroring needs), our motivations to merge with omnipotent figures and feel caught up in their greatness (expressions of our self's idealization-merger needs), or our desires to congregate with others just like ourselves and to protect the uniqueness of our identity (expressions of our self's alter-ego needs). Primarily through Kohut are we learning to accept our narcissistic strivings, just as we have learned though Freud to accept our sexual strivings. Loosely stated, through Kohut's work "self-love" (healthy narcissism of the self) is elevated to a status equal to that of "object love" (love of others).

From the point of view of group psychology or psychohistory, Kohut's most important methodological and conceptual step was to consider the group self as analogous to the individual self. Insights into the central core of the self were expanded by Kohut into the realm of group or cultural life. Groups have the same narcissistic needs for mirroring, idealizing, and alteregoing responses, and the same proclivity for fragmentation, depression, and rage as characteristic of the individual. The more vulnerable the group's self-cohesion (the more inadequately formed the nuclear self of the group) the more sensitive to ridicule, rejection, and criticism, and the more inclined to fragmentation, withdrawal, and rageful reactions. The concept of the group self allows us to see whether a group is developing near its optimal capacity, is able to utilize available selfobject support, and is moving on to fulfill its ideals, or whether it has been seriously injured, is unable to utilize mature selfobjects, and thus is regressively engaged in activities of narcissistic rage or isolation.

A tremendously illuminating insight into the power and presence of selfobject relationships also emerges. Selfobject relationships are not restricted just to therapy settings, nor merely characteristic of persons with disorders of the self, nor simply the archaic, but necessary, needs of childhood development. Kohut adamantly affirms that supporting selfobject relationships are necessary for all of us throughout all our life. Every individual needs the mirroring, idealizing, and alteregoing responses of selfobject others. We never outgrow these needs. They are as psychologically essential as air for our body. Without them we not only emotionally perish, we may even physically perish—personally, as well as a cultural group.

From this awareness of the ubiquitous need for selfobject responsiveness developed Kohut's most crucial observation-proposition of all. Kohut stresses that the normative, primary, central psychological relationship of all human life is the experience of the relationship between the self and its selfobjects, the "self-selfobject" relationship. The deepest level to be reached, the bedrock of our psychological existence, is that of the more or less empathic responses of the self's selfobjects, and the repercussions upon and responses by the self to its selfobjects. The self has life only in the air of its selfobject milieu. There is, therefore, no baby in isolation, no middle-aged person in isolation, no congregation in isolation, no family group in isolation. There is always the person or group surrounded by the complex network of their responding, nonresponding, or defectively responding selfobjects.

The self of an individual or group emerges from and takes shape by means of this environment of selfobjects and their more or less empathic responses. This is the psychological foundation for the unfolding of our self. From it springs our philosophical and spiritual affirmations of life's hope or its despair. From it issues our tendencies for broad encompassing empathy for others or our tendencies for cold detachment, if not destructive rage. The essential restoration of human relationships is essentially the restoration of self-selfobject relationships. Any serious effort to understand and help individuals or groups must necessarily grasp the power and presence of the self-selfobject context of life.

The preservation of the self was considered paramount by Kohut, a position I and others affirm. His axiomatic value was that of helping humankind maintain a life of meaning by advancing empathic selfobject responsiveness to one's self and to the selves of others. For Kohut, our human survival rests upon healthy development of our empathic self-selfobject relationships. Moved by these values, and embracing self psychological insight into the nature of our narcissistic strivings, I endeavor to analyze the selves of two whom many of us hold personally precious and culturally indispensable: pastors and parishes.

Chapter 3

MIRRORING, IDEALIZING, AND ALTEREGO NEEDS OF PASTORS

There are two implicit foci in this attempt to analyze the "narcissistic struggles of pastors and parishes." On the one hand is an endeavor to describe the character and dynamics of ministers' self-struggles and of churches' self-struggles (how unfulfilled or distorted grandiose-mirroring, idealization-merger, or alterego needs shape the psychological makeup of each). On the other hand is an effort to elucidate how particular, prominent narcissistic needs of ministers encountering particular, cardinal narcissistic orientations of congregations give rise to a wide variety of pastor-parish struggles between them. In this chapter we are engaged in the first half of that first enterprise as we consider narcissistic struggles of pastors.

A central theme repeatedly accented is that an empathic selfobject milieu is the precondition of a good life—from childhood to old age. There are pastors who experience that they are leading meaningful, joyful, creative lives despite the presence of physical and psychological suffering. Conversely, there are clergypersons in all denominations who experience leading joyless, nonfulfilling, empty lives despite their obvious success and the absence of physical or economic pain. The key determiner as to whether or not a pastor is able to be enlivened by personal goals, uplifted by cherished ideals, or assured of communal belonging is the degree to which the self of the pastor is experienced as essentially firm, vigorous, and harmonious, and the degree to which the pastor is surrounded by an atmosphere of empathically resonating selfobjects currently available, cherishingly remembered, or worshipfully imaged.

When the self of a pastor is defectively structured, weak, or disharmonious, the pastor is extremely vulnerable to blows to his self-cohesion and attendant self-esteem. Real or imagined injuries result in shamefaced withdrawal and/or narcissistic rage. While such efforts are often disruptive to ongoing human relationships, the continual intense need for selfobject responses, and the withdrawal and rage resultant when expected selfobject responses fail, are signs that the pastor is striving mightily to reengage the developmental process toward stable self-cohesion. At the very least, these disruptive narcissistic reactions may be healthy in that they represent attempts by the pastor to hold on to whatever remnant of his self is still intact. A severe crisis arises when the pastor loses all hope, loses even a minimal capacity to "hang in there."

In the last chapter I indicated that there is a spectrum of narcissistic needs and demands that corresponds to the cohesiveness of the individual (Tables 1, 2, & 3). At the one extreme are archaic selfobject needs; at the other are transformed, healthy selfobject needs. The pastors I describe in this and following chapters suffer from defective or inadequately structured selves. As a consequence, their self-cohesion is vulnerable and prone to fragmentation.

Furthermore, their narcissistic needs and selfobject

expectations have yet to become transformed and maturated; i.e., they still show signs of being developmentally archaic or regressive. My central effort throughout these pages is to provide a "feel" for the presence and power of particular narcissistic needs in the lives of pastors and parishes, rather than to show the process of therapy or to support the perspective of self psychology via example. Consequently, I offer clinical vignettes of self-struggles in pastors and parishes rather than full-blown case histories.[1]

CENTRALITY OF GRANDIOSE-MIRRORING NEEDS

Rev. Alan S. was a warm and witty pastor. He loved God and he cared for his church. Despite all outwardly apparent personal and professional success, however, he suffered privately from a pervasive sense of doubt and emptiness. Often nothing really seemed to matter to him, even though he continued to work and serve others. Purposes and ideals would animate his body and mind for a short while, and then collapse, leaving him vacant, uncertain, and feeling extremely alone. When he came for therapy, physical zest, intellectual interests, and spiritual sensitivities were minimal.

"I have wrestled with despondency most of my life," he began. "I have never felt sure of myself as a person, at least not for very long." In particular, he had always dreaded any occasion where he might feel put down, laughed at, or rejected, no matter how slight or unintended it might be. This dread of personal mortification was accompanied by an opposite, private longing. For as far back as he could remember, he had always yearned for the bright, beaming benedictions of others upon all that he did and said. Praise from others was an "elixir," as he called it, that washed away all doubt and filled him with an intoxicating certainty of his capacities and unique specialness.

Indeed, at these times his considerable physical and intellectual attributes did flourish. In the absence of continu-
ously received admiring responses, however, the doubt and
vulnerability to criticism quickly returned. His "antenna,"
consequently, was always out for how others were responding to him, and what signals he received determined
the state of his self-esteem and self-assurance.

If his sermons or his suggestions were met with admiring, enthusiastic approval by his congregation, for example, he would feel a flush of well-being, and his commitment to his work would again become firm. On the
other hand, when praise for his Sunday sermon was sparse
or perfunctory as he shook parishioners' hands at the door,
or when consistory members complained about aspects of
his ministry that needed attention, he alternated between
deep despair and intense rage. He constructed revenge
fantasies in his mind, picturing how "they" would be sorry
if he packed up and left them, and how "they" would really
have to suffer under a minister less capable and thoughtful
than he.

At times he would even contemplate suicide, both as
a means of escape from his feelings of belittlement and
hurt, and as an expression of his rage at those who had
injured him by being so insensitive to his hard work and
refined skills. While in the past he had been able, more or
less, to present an external image of calmness, self-giving,
and openness to others, this outward demeanor was dan-
gerously beginning to crumble.

Keeping himself together had always been a struggle,
but an accumulation of narcissistic injuries (from his wife
and parishioners primarily), coupled with narcissistic disappointments in his body (impotence), decimated what self-
cohesion he had been able to retain. The old emptiness
and doubts began to overwhelmed him as narcissistic tensions increased. Church duties started to slide. His irritation
when others did not respond as he expected surfaced in

Bible study groups and in consistory meetings. Normal appreciation failed to satisfy or soothe him. He was like a man with a hole in his toe, he never got filled up. Praise, thanks, acknowledgements, and acquiescences all ran out of him and he needed, demanded (subtly and not so subtly) more. Clinically stated, the increase in narcissistic tensions from a variety of sources was threatening the very integrity (cohesiveness) of his self-structure. His already vulnerable self lacked a solid inner core around and from which he could maintain his equilibrium when alone, or when others failed to provide those admiring-confirming responses he so desperately required.

In order to counteract the excruciating feeling of emptiness inside, and to armor himself against the dread of mortifying injuries that seemed always to pursue him, he began to look for experiences that could decisively stimulate and empower him. They came in the form of novel and dangerous sexual activities. Pastoral relations with females took on a seductive quality. He urged the disclosure of intimate sexual secrets in a "growth" group made up entirely of women parishioners. These stimulating sexual fantasies and subtle voyeuristic acts soon gave way to more livid involvements.

For the first time in this very upright man's life, he entered into a sexual affair—with a woman from the congregation. The meetings were frequent, and in places where detection was highly possible. She was not particularly beautiful, but she clearly conveyed to him just how wonderful a man he was to her. She literally gave herself to him body and soul, resonating with his anger at the church, protecting him, applauding his every idea. During these times with her he felt wondrously alive. Physical strength and emotional confidence surged once again through body organs. His mind filled with new ideas and images. A sense of regained well-being flooded him, as did tears of relief at being "raised from the dead." Although he knew his actions were inappropriate, he felt minimal guilt or sin. "Some days I'd sell my soul for a hug," he confided quietly.

For this modern Faust, the focus on sexuality as the epicenter of his existence expressed the fragmentation of his self-structure. Rather than being smoothly integrated into the functioning of a cohesive body-mind-spirit-self, sex arose in its explosive intensity as a kind of disintegration product from a disintegrating self. On the one hand, therefore, this sexual acting out expressed that Rev. Alan S. was falling apart; that is, his self-cohesion was splitting up, resulting in sexual drives arising as isolated fragments, running wildly without integration into, and limits set by, an intact functioning self. On the other hand, however, it is important to understand that the sexual activities were also desperate attempts to hold the self together. What remnant of self-structure Rev. Alan S. had was carried by and at least minimally preserved by this splintered dimension of his personality. Efforts toward restoration as well as expressions of self-fragmentation were operative in the sexual franticness.

As we worked together in therapy, it became clear that he longed for more than a sexual embrace *per se;* he longed for a saving embrace that would heal his self's emptiness. Sex was but a momentary, remedial attempt to keep the self stimulated, alive, and functional. Moreover, sex represented the persistent attempt of his self to fill in for crucially missing selfobject responses in his past.

Early childhood memories poured out, and from them we were able to make broad genetically based reconstructions of chronic attitudes in his home. He recalled how his mother was never emotionally available to him. She seemed always preoccupied with her housework and inner thoughts. Later, as an adult, he realized that she was a severely depressed individual. In her self-absorption she did not embrace her son with admiring eyes, did not cradle him in a hug that told him how special he was to her, did not let her face shine upon him and be gracious to him with a glowing smile that he could carry supportingly with him all his life long.

His father, unfortunately, was not physically or emotionally available either for the necessary mirroring responses Alan needed for the development of healthy self-esteem and for the consolidation of his self. Alan remembered with great pain the time he excitedly told of his call to go into the ministry, only to have his businessman father openly ridicule the decision. Neither could the father present himself as an empathically available idealized figure with whom Alan as a boy could merge, share his father's specialness, and thus compensate for his mother's lack of mirroring ministrations. The absence of the mother's life-sustaining mirroring responses was coupled with the father's inadequate ability to present himself as a figure for idealization.

From this disturbed self-selfobject family context, Alan's self-cohesion emerged weak and vulnerable. Instead of enjoying the visceral assurance of being whole and continuous, fully alive and vigorous, balanced and harmonious, he experienced emptiness and fragmentation, lack of zestful energy, and general disarray. Instead of being able to sustain or regulate his own self-esteem, or to utilize the normal appreciations extended to him, he was left with a persistent, archaic need for constant acclaim and recognition, which he desperately required in order to ward off the deadness and disharmony within his self.

The archaic need for the cohesion-firming responses of mirroring selfobjects to his grandiose self pervaded his personality and pastoral life. In the therapy relationship, as I provided a receptive atmosphere in which his grandiose-mirroring needs were empathically understood and accepted, the demands of his self for affirming selfobject responses, and the intensity of his narcissistic rage at unfeeling others, were slowly disclosed. In a process sustained over time by his experience of me as a reliable, mirroring selfobject, and aided by empathic explanations regarding his reactions to narcissistic injuries, the disintegration of his self abated, and psychological energies slowly began to be mobilized productively toward restoration of his self. Such efforts were painful and tentative. Very gradually, however, signs of vitalized self-cohesion emerged. He sensed at times a new feeling of internal solidness. He was pleased with his increasing ability to "stay level," even when his wife would get angry at him, or his sermons failed to receive sparkling acclaim.

Furthermore, rather than fume in frustration, he found himself able to approach difficult situations without feeling that his own self-esteem was on the line. Empathy for others also increased, along with the capacity to laugh at himself. Thoughtfully he spoke to the female parishioner, relinquished the sexual nature of their relationship, and tried to help her through the narcissistic injuries he had caused her. A new vitality for his work emerged. The future seemed brighter, open, and he entered a chaplaincy program at a local hospital.

While I do not intend to discuss here the restoration process via therapy, a particularly delightful dream he reported late in our work indicated both the centrality of his mirroring needs and the way in which the intensity of this selfobject need was becoming healthily modified. A transformation of his archaic grandiose-mirroring need was underway. He dreamed that God was sitting behind a desk in heaven, dressed in a brown business suit. When Alan entered the room, God looked up, recognized instantly who it was, and, with a pleased smile, calling him by name, promptly came around the desk to warmly shake Alan's hand. The dream was a religious experience for the pastor even though we both could laugh at its gentle humor. Narcissistically interpreted, God was now more firmly anchored as a mirroring selfobject upon whom Alan could count. *God* at least knew his name, and would make *His* face to shine upon him with admiration and recognition. In this reliably empathic bond with the divine, mirroring selfobject God, the minister's self-esteem and self-cohesiveness became more consistently firm. Assurance of God's grace in his life empowered him. His ministry in all dimensions deepened in understanding and in zest.

Of course, vestiges of unfulfilled human mirroring needs were represented in the dream as well, and yet the dream imagery suggested that these narcissistic needs were being fulfilled in new, transformed ways. The image of God in a business suit reminded both of us of his businessman father. The businessman-God now carried in part those confirming, mirroring responses Rev. Alan S. required in general from his father, and that admiring response to his call to the ministry which he required specifically from his father. Similarly, God's smile, recognition, and physical touch now carried and partially filled in for his mother's absent mirroring ministrations. On the health-maintaining side, the God-dream also condensed all those reliable selfobject responses Alan had been fortunate to experience throughout his life, particularly those of a warm, encouraging pastor in his youth, a chaplain at college who took him under his wing, and those of his present therapist who, dressed often in a business suit, regularly arose to meet him with an attentive greeting.

That God provided a sense of well-being for this pastor through the agency of being a mirroring selfobject support did not diminish the dream's spiritual significance for Alan, and rightly so. Something new was happening. A transformation of his archaic need for mirroring sustenance was occurring; it had not merely been displaced upon a cosmic selfobject figure. Alan still needed healthy mirroring responses from his church and others, but he required them with less intensity, directness, and perfection. His self's well-being was sustained more now by the memory of other's admiration for him, by common comments of appreciation given him, and by his own capacities healthily to admire himself and to regulate his own self-esteem. To know others were "for him" supported him in the absence of direct mirroring acclaim. Consequently, he was less devastated when injured in some way, and his own empathy for others' selfobject yearnings broadened. His increased self-assurance, and his more sensitive pastoral involvements with parishioners, were a joy to him—and to his therapist.

Let us shift now to another pastor, who I shall refer to as Rev. Jeffrey W. The narcissistic focus of Jeff's life was similar to Alan's with defects in self-structure occurring around the grandiose-mirroring needs of the self. Rev. Jeffrey W. came to therapy with a particular goal in mind, and that was to reflect on whether or not he should stay in the ministry. He was "tired of casting pearls before swine," he stated, bitterly. As he began to tell his story, it seemed his anger at the church was justified. He was outraged, for example, when his well-thought out directives for church rituals, such as communion, baptism, and marriage, were met with the consistory's response, "This is just your opinion." The injury to his self-esteem was heightened even more, and consequently the intensity of his narcissistic rage, when parishioners called upon former pastors for support of their position over his, or when the consistory voted to allow former ministers to perform ceremonies in the church at which Rev. Jeffrey W. would not officiate.

On further investigation, however, we found that he had a long history of vague, deep, knot-in-the-stomach anxiety that he could not explain, along with an intense impatience with his parishioners (and with his wife and children). In fact, he had once been asked to leave a church he served because he seemed unresponsive to their needs. While confessing sadly to me that much of the time he "bungled through life," without thinking how others were feeling or what he himself was feeling, he still could not shake a militant, I'm-in-charge posture. "I want them to get on the stick, hop to it, be perfect, to know the truth and do it!"

While he generally hid from others these demands for in-line adherence to the truth and practices as he espoused them, he did not disavow his own grandiosity and need for grandiose acclaim. With a flourish he had written on his sermon notebook, when he first arrived, the words from Ezekiel, "O dry bones, hear the word of the Lord!" He would be the prophet of the Lord who brought life to these rattling dry bones of a church!

We began to understand together how his own dry bones yearned for resurrection through the breath of admiring, mirroring responses of selfobject parishioners (and family members). When the psychological oxygen of these mirroring responses to his self was absent or minimal, he was filled with great apprehension (the "foreboding of some great yet nameless danger," as he defined it), and with narcissistic rage (that wanted to do away with those so stupid). The cohesion of his self was extremely fragile and prone to fragmentation. When, for example, a parishioner complained about his selection of a particular hymn, Jeff felt "like a whale who bleeds and then is attacked by everything." This description poignantly touched the chasm of vulnerability that lay beneath the demand for grandiose-mirroring responses.

Yet while he contemplated leaving "those people" in the church, he was frightened to do so; not from lack of secular work skills nor the threat of financial collapse, but for a powerful narcissistic reason. "I feel I have my superego connected with God, and if I'm doing God's work full-time, then I am worthy, acceptable, special. But I'm not special if I get down in the muck of a secular job." God would apparently deem him worthy, make His face to shine upon the pastor and fulfill the pastor's yearning for special recognition, only as long as he remained in God's milieu, the church. All other areas of life were psychological death, even though theologically he knew this was indefensible. Whereas Rev. Alan S.'s dream of being connected with God as the divine, mirroring selfobject represented a transformation of his archaic narcissistic need, the partial resolution of traumatic selfobject failures in Alan's past, and the establishment of a symbolic, spiritual memory that brought self-cohesion, Rev. Jeffrey W.'s vision of the divine continued to express fear of recurring traumatic selfobject reactions.

With great anxiety he told of his utter despair when contemplating that there might be an emptiness in the cosmos, of God being absent. "If that were so, I couldn't go on." Later he linked this despair of divine absence with painful memories of his own father who, although acting godlike in his utter domination of the home, was often gone from his son physically and emotionally. Jeff had waited for the self-confirming word of his father's praise, which seldom came; had waited for his father's expressed joy at being with his son, utterance of which was lukewarm or cold. "Even when I was with him, he wasn't really with me."

Jeff eventually sought in God the fulfillment of his narcissistic yearning for a life-enhancing, mirroring presence. Traumatic self-selfobject experiences in his childhood, however, left him vulnerable and uncertain even in his relationship to the heavenly Father to whom he had transferred his hope for mirroring restoration.

Whereas Alan's illicit, uncharacteristic sexual affair was an expression of his fragmentation, on the one hand, and of his desperate, remedial attempt to keep the self alive and functioning, on the other, Jeff's fragmentation as well as attempt to maintain a residual self were manifest through the elevation of his intellect. Efforts to maintain any semblance of self-esteem, any stability in life, were primarily centered in the functions and activities of his mind.

To reason, to reason rightly, and to have others swayed by that reason, carried and preserved what remnant of self he still retained. Alan's self became eroticized; Jeff's self became intellectualized. Consequently, to ignore, criticize, or reject instances of his intellect—his plans, programs, or perceptions—was to demean him totally. This intellectual self-remnant preserving function, however, was split off from the emotion-sensing, empathic-resonance dimension of his self, and thus he "bungled through," as he said, insensitive to others' feelings and to his own.

In therapy, however, I did not accuse him of "performing" or of "being intellectual." His intellectualizing was not a resistance against being human. Self psychologically understood, his intellectualizing was a decided achievement of early life, and an invaluable asset of his personality that had elicited some recognition from his parents, and had protected him somewhat from unempathic selfobject responses. While fragmented and isolated, his intellectualizing safeguarded the maintenance of his self.

The restoring words he needed were not interpretations of his defensiveness or directives for him to "get in touch with your feelings." The life-enhancing words needed were those that expressed understanding and acceptance of his demands for intellectual dominance, and that empathically interpreted how, in moments of selfobject abandonment, latching on to his own mind and thought as if his life depended upon it was, indeed, psychologically true.

In their daily lives and in their individual therapies, Rev. Alan S. and Rev. Jeff W. were engaged in narcissistic selfobject relations other than mirroring ones. Idealizations of various intensities and forms sustained Alan at crucial points in his personal development, for example. Jeff searched for a church composed of like-minded individuals who would alterego his own intellectual approach to theology and ministry. While both clergymen were typical in expressing various narcissistic needs and aims, their selves, as with all of us, congealed around a central narcissistic aspect. In their case, grandiose-mirroring selfobject responses were dominant in the maintenance and enhancement of their selves, and shaped in large measure their interactions with others.

Other ministers, however, are less insistent than these two on receiving life sustaining grandiose-mirroring responses of praise and admiration, even though they desperately need them. Rev. Kate G., for instance, a minister in a pastoral counseling program, quietly kept her "successes" with counseled patients to herself, lest she "lose them" to colleagues' criticisms. While she longed for others to "celebrate" her accomplishments, her great fear that others would find them trivial, or show lack of empathic resonance with her own quiet joy, kept her silent and reactively hypercritical of her genuinely outstanding work. Another minister quietly asked God to place upon his shoulders "the mantle of famous theologians when they die."

Pastors also disavow or repress their own grandiose-mirroring needs and their expressions of narcissistic rage. Rev. David F. in the "second-best church" whom we encounter in the Introduction, for example, disavowed his archaic grandiose demands and narcissistic rage. Respect was simply due him as a minister, and his revenge was justified in the light of the malevolent treatment he received. He was totally unforgiving in his criticism of the church. He became irritated when he felt I spoke about the congregation with a degree of objectivity; that is, as a group also suffering from injuries to its self, rather than as villains who were trying to destroy him. A rigid wall of disavowal, that is, a vertical split between his recognized, intense action and its emotional, internal meaning, kept him protected from further narcissistic injury. Unfortunately, it also kept him in a state of fragmentation that was ruining his health, his family, and his ministry.

Another pastor exhibited a patronizing attitude wrapped in graciousness that reeked of condescension. The grandiosity of his manner, however, he completely repressed. Here a horizontal split existed, that is, his consciousness was cut off from even an awareness of his behavior, let alone its unconscious meaning.

We are all familiar, as well, with the elicitation of mirroring acclaim through endured suffering or self-depreciation. A pastor who come for an emergency therapy session stressed his need to confess before the collected congregation the self-centeredness of his ways. "I think just before the call to commitment would be the most moving and memorable time," he said, with barely disguised satisfaction at the imagined impression. As I got to know his story, he reminded me of a fellow in Franz Kafka's haunting piece, *Conversation with the Supplicant.* The narrator tells of a time he went to church every day and noticed there a young fellow who had thrown his whole lean length along the floor. Every now and then the fellow would clutch his head and, sighing loudly, would beat it in his upturned palms on the stone flags. A few old women in the church watched the young man at his devotions. Their awareness of him seemed to please him, for before each of his pious outbursts he cast his eyes around to see whether many of them were looking. Later in the story, when the supplicant is confronted by the storyteller, he offers a reason for his need to make people look at him in church: "There has never been a time in which I have been convinced from within myself that I am alive."[2] Similar words have been uttered by pastors plagued by disintegration anxiety, that threat of emptiness which seeks assuagement through the attentive mirroring responses of others to the self's mortification.

Finally, although the narcissistic despondencies and rages of Rev. Alan S. and Rev. Jeff W. were more blatantly experienced and expressed, there is a wide spectrum of such narcissistic reactions to selfobject failure. Narcissistic depression/depletion in a milder form may materialize in the "burned out" feeling of a still caring pastor. Narcissistic rage in a milder form may be manifest in a pastor's passive regard for the congregation, a distant politeness that follows through with the letter of ministry but lacks the spirit. Some pastors, furthermore, are marked by chronic narcissistic depletion or rage, rather than by acute, temporary narcissistic depletion or rage following momentary, limited disappointments in selfobject responses.

Narcissistic rage in its wide variety of forms may be directed toward the self as well as at others. While Rev. Alan S.'s suicide thoughts, for example, emanated from a depleted, empty self, suicide is also contemplated and enacted as an expression of intense rage at one's self for being stupid, wishy-washy, or unheroic; in short, for narcissistic injuries the person has caused to his self. The general point to be made here is that just as anything can be the means through which grandiose-mirroring claims and needs are expressed, so, too, are there innumerable expressions of narcissistic rage and depletion. In attempting to comprehend these self psychological struggles in the lives of pastors and of parishes, we must not look for external resemblances only, but also for similarity of function among what might appear as disparate actions and attitudes. As stated earlier, the clinical vignettes offered here of pastors Alan S., Jeffrey W., and others are intended to give a "feel" for the presence and power of grandiose-mirroring needs—operative to some extent in the life of us all.

CENTRALITY OF IDEALIZATION-MERGER NEEDS

Self psychology illuminates the indispensable nature of healthy selfobject responses for the consolidation of the self. The healthy self, in turn, makes efficient use of selfobjects, and acquires new internal structures by finding new routes toward inner completeness.[3] Furthermore, in a healthy self, at least one aspect of the self is able to function well; that is, the grandiose-mirroring aspect, the idealizing-merger aspect, or the alterego aspect serves as the sustaining center shaping the unfolding of the self's personality, goals, and relationships. Combinations of these three may also provide shape and substance to the self. Generally, however, the self tends to become focused—healthily or pathologically—around a particular narcissistic configuration. That central configuration may be a primary self-structure or a compensatory self-structure.

The original, *primary* set of narcissistic responses by selfobject parents may be especially strong and structurally enhancing, leading to a healthy self formed around purposes and goals reflecting mature extensions of this original self-selfobject matrix. In my own case, for example, the strong, consistent mirroring responses from my mother have led me to a lifelong, primary reliance upon remembered and current mirroring reactions for the maintenance of my self-esteem and self-cohesion. They have led me, as well, to engage in activities that, although motivated in part by the example of idealized others and formed somewhat by empathic sensitivity to the needs of alteregos, are principally expected to elicit selfobject approval and support.

I am, as a consequence, more sensitive to grandiose-mirroring injuries than to idealization-merger or alterego injuries. Thus, when I once received a sizable check for an article I had written, the joy at receiving the recognition was dampened when I read a line written to me by the editor. I had begun the article with an episode from the life of a renowned individual, and then insightfully (I thought) elaborated upon its message for pastors. The editor commented: "The real strength of this piece is its opening anecdote, of course, and we feel the application that follows might be shortened a bit without hurting the impact." I have resisted writing him back suggesting that he be more careful in how he treats the self-esteem of his contributors.

Kohut has shown that a developing self also congeals around selfobject *compensations*. When, for example, a mother's mirroring presence is absent or flawed, the child may turn developmentally toward idealization of and merging with the (omnipotent) father, who, it is hoped, can present himself as a selfobject figure the child can admire. If the powerful enough father empathically resonates with the child's need to merge with him, the child feels lifted up into the father's calmness and self-assurance, which is eventually "transmuted" into the child's own stable self-structure, i.e., becomes a part of the person's ongoing internal capacities for self-soothing and comforting. We saw how this unfortunately did not happen with Rev. Alan S.[4] Similarly, sound, supportive alterego relationships can compensate, more or less, for weak or inconsistent mirroring and idealizing selfobject presences, leading to activities of the self that foster self-sustenance through involvements with homogeneous others.

Compensations also occur commonly in life as temporary means for restoration of self-esteem and self-cohesion. For example, a pastor who prided herself on her perspicacity was shattered when she learned that her husband had long been unfaithful to her. In a burst of effort to regain her equilibrium and internal self-esteem (formerly sustained by grandiose-mirroring responses and self-enhancing mirroring fantasies regarding herself), she withdrew into prolonged meditation, seeking blissful merger with omniscient God. That is, she relied temporarily upon an intense idealizing selfobject-bonding to curtail her self's depletion and restore its former firmness.

The folkloric saying that "misery loves company" has its narcissistic foundation in this inclination to soothe one's self by seeking the companionship of similarly suffering alteregos. These narcissistic compensations are usually temporary. Over the years, however, they may become permanent, characterologic traits. Much depends upon the availability of primary and substitute selfobjects, the depth of their empathic resonance, and the self's inherent vulnerabilities and strengths. Constitutional, developmental, family, and cultural factors, therefore, all play a role in the way the self is organized around a particular narcissistic orientation, and the way the self tends to seek compensation for selfobject injuries.

For whatever reason, primary or compensatory in nature, idealization-merger needs are strong among clergy. At a pastors' retreat I once lead, clergy began to speak on the theme of confirming their call to the ministry by effusive expressions of gratitude for those special individuals who had supported and guided them at crucial personal-spiritual points in their lives. The whole tone of the descriptions left no doubt that these remembered individuals were highly idealized. I reflected back to the pastors the nature of the powerful statements they were making, namely that their capacity for sustained work and spiritual aliveness rested in this experience of being lifted up into the reassuring strength of those special others. I offered a line from a lovely song to catch the mood of their hearts: "If I can fly higher than eagles, then you are the wind beneath my wings."

Tears flowed. Pastors remember and yearn for idealized individuals with whom they can feel an intimate part, in and with whose perceived strength, wisdom, and undaunted values they can feel united, reassured, lifted up. Many a minister carries out a committed, caring ministry through the support of past and present involvements with inspiring, idealized selfobject figures, human as well as divine.

When so engaged, a minister can resonate with the words of St. Paul: "I can do all things in him who strengthens me." Empowerment here issues from a sense of being embraced by and vitally one with omnipotent God. Paul's grandiosity ("I can do all things") is based upon a central idealizing-merger selfobject relationship ("in him who strengthens me"). We see here, perhaps, the psychological substrata of grace: the infusion of grace enters into the human self through the power of narcissistic relationships with empathic, vitalizing selfobject presences, human and divine. For pastors so sustained, they are essentially able to "run the race and not get weary." Not all ministers are so fortunate, however. We turn now to consider pastors whose struggles are centered in weakness and deficiencies in this idealization-merger sector of their selves. We consider, first, examples of intense self-selfobject disturbances, followed by instances of more benign merger needs.

For much of his adult life, Rev. Steve K. had been in and out of contact with a remarkably wide variety of therapists. In each relationship he held out great hope that the therapist would relieve him of his persistent problems. In each relationship, he was disappointed. They could not convince him of, or even offer to him, "the truth" he sought. They lacked the "magical power" he need to purge his despised self and disperse the ominous clouds of doom closing over him.

He was, as he described himself, "filled with shit, garbage, junk. I am polluted, crammed with crappy cobwebs, dirt, and evil-smelling things. And I want to be washed whiter than snow, as the Bible promises is possible." He castigated himself for his adolescent masturbation, his current sexual thoughts, his cowardice in the face of danger, his fear of dying, his weakness at not being able to let go of his difficulties, the emptiness of his faith, and his mistrust of himself, others, and God. All these made him vile and wretched. The intensity of his self-denigration reminded me of Rev. Arthur Dimmesdale in *The Scarlet Letter,* who considered himself "the vilest of all sinners."[5] The crucial difference was that Rev. Arthur Dimmesdale's guilt arose out of genuinely grievous "sins," while Rev. Steve K.'s self-reproaches arose from insidious feelings that he was "shit." He yearned to be made "new and whole inside, right now, magically," but he greatly feared he would never emerge pure and peaceful. A powerfully depressive mood lodged within him.

Data from therapy suggested that Steve K.'s excessive self-incriminations were due to weaknesses in his self-structure. On the one hand, his self-critical attitude lacked smoothness. It did not appear to be a reflective, moral function integrated fittingly into the wholeness of a cohesively functioning self. Regardless of how terrible he was or was not, he displayed an inability to keep his feelings of guilt and the resultant self-reproaches within moderate, realistic limits. Self-vindictiveness ran as wild as Alan S.'s sexual drives.

On the other hand, he also lacked the internal capacity for self-soothing, as well as the capacity for internalizing the reassuring comfort offered by others. Unbridled self-criticism dominated his thinking, inhibited creative, productive work, and thwarted possibilities for intimately supporting relationships. From the perspective of self psychology, this impulse for self-incrimination stood as a disintegration product of Steve K.'s fragmenting self. Whereas Alan S.'s precariously cohesive self had become eroticized, and Jeff W.'s remnant self had become intellectualized, Steve K.'s fragmented self became moralized.

The surmise that his hypercritical attitude emanated from narcissistic difficulties found support also in the nature of his restoration fantasies. He would become "whiter than snow," not through punishment or penitence, not through vicarious atonements, but rather by being "lifted up into truth," embraced by those with "magical powers," immersed with God in projects of "cosmic purpose." Restoration of his vile self would come through these purifying merger states with powerful, absolute-truth-holding, idealized selfobject healers.

The fantasized goals of restoration, furthermore, were

not for the achievement of grandiose power on his part, nor for the admiring acclaim of others, but rather for the goals of inner peace and the reassuring harmony of his thinking, feeling, acting, and believing. Stated more clinically, his weak and defectively structured self called for merger with an archaic, omnipotent idealized selfobject in order to ward off further deterioration of his self-cohesion, and in order to return to the process of healthy self-development.

Slowly, we pieced together the psychogenetic background of his fragmented world. Like his fellow clergy, Alan and Jeff, Steve also experienced an ominous, unnamed threat-to-being hanging over him. "When I awake in the morning, I don't want to get out of bed. This gray, menacing fog descends around me, encapsulating me. I just want to pull the covers over my head and hide." When I gently wondered what he thought was going to happen to him, he began to shake. Wrapping his arms around himself, he blurted out, "Somehow it's going to destroy me!" The vulnerability of his very existence, his feeling of unprotectedness, left him panic-stricken.

The existential menacing fog, and his wish, as an adult, to hide under the covers, were nearly total redramatizations of a recurring traumatic childhood episode. He recalled, with relived panic, the many, many nights he would hide under his covers trying to block out the fights of his alcoholic parents. "When they were outside tearing one another apart, I was being torn apart inside," he recalled. This is a poignant expression of a basic psychological fact: the missing, firming functions of selfobjects and the missing firmness of a self are one and the same thing. His life "lacked integration," as he said, and was "out of harmony," due to the disintegrated and disharmonious milieu of his parental selfobjects. Preoccupied with themselves, filled with their own narcissistic rage, they were unable to provide for their son that narcissistic context necessary for the smooth development of a well-integrated self.

More particularly, their unavailability as soothing, composing, idealized selfobjects resulted in deficiencies in their son's ability to calm and comfort himself. The pathogenic faults and failings of Steve K.'s inadequately responding selfobjects lead to pathogenic faults and failings in the formation of his own self-structure. It should be said, however, in a spirit of empathic understanding, that the self-stunting reactions of his parents most likely stemmed from narcissistic difficulties they themselves were suffering. A disenhancing psychological heritage, consequently, was being passed on from generation to generation.

During these early childhood years, no healthy selfobject substitutes seemed available to step into the breach and supply Steve with needed narcissistic sustenance, either through mirroring responses, other idealizing relationships, or alterego support. The all-powerful, idealized selfobjects developmentally needed by the child remained a need unmodified in his adult life. Disappointments in idealized others he had temporarily turned to exacerbated the need, as well as the fearful doubt of ever being soothed. Only an idealized object of unquestioned superiority, who held "the truth" and would purify him by lifting him up into it for him to share, could assuage his long mistrust, and fulfill the ancient yearning for perfect peace.

His search for an omniscient, idealized healer began to show signs of severe narcissistic regression. Energy was withdrawn from ordinary human involvements and devoted to an inner, ethereal world, where his archaic, unmet needs for selfobject merger focused heavily upon cosmic figures and forces. He became "supernaturally inclined." Accounts of being thrown against the wall by "the evil eye" were reported, as well as long hours of meditation where he sat in the presence of God. When a parishioner tried to quell his relentless self-criticism by saying that Satan was vying for his soul, he sensed a calmness descending over him.

"I am in battle with the devil, and I know I'm not going

to win, but I am going out to make a valiant, courageous try, expecting, during it all, to be the receptacle of God's grace and power in this futile process of my struggle." While there certainly were elements of his grandiose self evident here, namely himself as the heroic, tragic figure, the underlying theme was that *someone* with omnipotent power was addressing him, *someone* was trying to make him theirs, whether God or the devil.

Considerations regarding the quality of the merger, or the character of the omnipotent figure, were lost in the urgency to restore a rapidly deteriorating self via some form of fusion with the archaic idealized selfobject. As the cure for his threatened self switched regressively to the supernatural realm, earthly agents became devalued, including those religious acts and rituals which for many individuals provide the means for sustained self-cohesion. Thus for the Rev. Steve K., worship, prayer, biblical study, and preaching became ever more empty.

It is important to stress that Steve was not psychotic; that is, the core of his self was not so defective or minimally functional that he had lost touch with reality. Self-disorders often result in symptoms that appear psychoticlike, but when carefully considered are found to be transitory, as assessed by the fact that in the face of consistent, empathic responses, the fragmenting of the individual's self is gradually halted, and the process of remobilization of the individual's self-development is begun—again. In contrast to severely psychotic individuals, those with narcissistic personality disorders have attained some degree of self-structure (albeit archaic and vulnerable), have constructed selfobject relationships, and therefore are protected from the serious threat of irreversible decompensation.

Yet quite clearly, this pastor was severely narcissistically disturbed. His self-cohesion was extremely weak (as signaled by his regression and fragmentation), and his ability to regulate tensions within himself and without was minimal. In this condition, his supernatural narcissistic gambit held serious consequences for him. If, at this cosmic plateau of gods and demons, there would be no dispersing of the foreboding fog, no purifying of his despised, "shitty" self, then further regression could occur. Such regression could involve hallucinations (archaic attempts at narcissistic fulfillment), cessation of personal self-care and human interactions (marked narcissistic depression/withdrawal), hypochondriasis, depersonalization, and derealization (structural fragmentation and disintegration), and the threat of suicide (in this case, the ultimate of self-directed narcissistic rage).

While this minister's narcissistic rage toward disappointing idealized selfobjects was guarded, and largely directed toward his own vilified self, Rev. Michael R., another minister in therapy with me, teemed with externalized narcissistic rage at flawed, idealized-cast selfobjects. Like his colleague, he also was looking for "the truth." "The truth," in this situation, however, was perceptive wisdom and pragmatic, technical know-how in the area of pastoral counseling. A deep vacancy of self-confidence within him called for a steady stream of advice, suggestions, and techniques he could use on patients he saw in the hospital.

In spite of his considerable training and adequate counseling capacities, he always felt himself an uncertain neophyte. He devoured book after book, attended workshop after workshop in the attempt to "fill myself up, to get it all under my belt." No matter how much poured in, it all seemed to leak out, and he turned, panic-stricken, to the wisdom of one idealized practitioner after another, in the effort to curb the sense of being weak, stupid, and ineffectual; in short, to bind up his vulnerable and fragmentation-prone self. What was more, he archly declared that others "ought" to confer upon him their acquired wisdom and skill. They had the expertise necessary for success. He yearned, and demanded, to be "baptized into their knowledge."

In a chaplaincy training program, for example, he literally shouted at the chaplain supervisor to tell him how to treat a particular patient on the floor, exclaiming that he *had* to know; that he was lost, uncertain, frantic, that unless the chaplain offered him ideas and insights into how he was to proceed, then he felt he had no choice but to give up his chaplaincy efforts all together.

When the supervisor failed to be a perfectly responding selfobject who initiated Michael R. into the "inner secrets" of those who know, then Michael was livid. At those times, his panic, mixed with rage, led him to paranoidlike reactions: "There's no one to understand or help me, not my parents, the world, the cosmos, or God! They are all SOBs who'll abandon me, victimize me. And I'm furious!" His intense suspiciousness and rage signaled the fragmenting of his self.

In an effort to reverse the painful disintegration of his self, and to reinstate some semblance of empowerment, he regressed into archaically grandiose sexual fantasies (imagining he had complete control over females who found him irresistible), and into regressive sexual behavior (becoming a neighborhood "peeping Tom," and engaging in prolonged periods of masturbation). Domination fantasies, voyeuristic activities, and hyperstimulation of his body were attempts to counteract his fragmentation through intense experiences of aliveness and strength. As we have seen before, sexuality represented both fragmentation as well as regressive efforts to reestablish a sense of self-unity. In terms of developmental needs, Michael R.'s archaic sexual activity, and the demand for idealized figures to "fill him up" ' with their knowledge, were attempts to compensate for those missing parts of his own self-structure.[6]

Not all idealization-merger needs are as intense or visible as Rev. Michael R.'s, of course. Often in therapy, such selfobject needs emerge very quietly. Rev. Jim P., for instance, indicated, almost as an aside, that he did not like to write out sermons. "Once the words are out of me they are not alive. I'm disconnected from them. They seem dead, and so do I when I speak what I've already written." He relished, instead, the experience of entering the pulpit with only background work and a prayer to God to finish what he had started. "It's an exhilarating experience, to see what comes forth." The creative process for him had to be fresh. When a new birth at each preaching-time occurred, Jim then felt the power and conviction of what he proclaimed. It was inspiring for him to think he could do this, and that somehow he and God were linked together in this ecclesiastical venture.

All clergy have had, or yearn for, something of this experience of being filled with the spirit when preaching. In many ways it can be an affirming occasion. In the Rev. Jim P.'s case, however, the repetitive structuring of the preaching situation so that this would happen, the intense, continuous need for an "alive feeling," the inability to experience satisfaction in and attachment to something that once was part of him but was "not him" once out of him, and the internal conviction of what he proclaimed only when it was divinely inspired—all this suggested a weakness in his self-structure. While there was a good deal of apparant grandiose satisfaction in Jim P.'s joint effort with God, the enhancement of his self and its empowerment came through the sense of being merged with God as the idealized selfobject. On the human plane, this mixture of grandiose power via idealization-merger lead this pastor to echo for himself the words of Jesus: "I and the Father are one."

CENTRALITY OF ALTEREGO NEEDS

Certain pastors have their creative-productive selves sustained by a milieu of expected or presently available mirroring selfobjects. Other pastors are predominantly sustained by feeling uplifted by idealized selfobjects and the ideals which emanate from them. Still other ministers derive the sustenance of their selves from being surrounded by alteregos; that is, they are nurtured by the abiding presence of others who are experienced as essentially like the pastors' selves.

Whether in archaic or mature forms, we have seen how the self psychologically appropriates others as extensions of its self (its selfobjects). In the alterego needs of the self, selfobjects are expected to function as a "twin" of the self, resonating with and echoing the self's own feelings, attitudes, skills, and talents. The self's experience of an adequately empathic alterego milieu is the narcissistic basis for the development of an assured sense of being "normal," and for the establishment of an abiding sense that the self "belongs." In general, then, adequate alteregoing also leads to firm self-cohesion.

The sense of not belonging often arises as the self fails to experience around it an atmosphere of alteregos. We have all experienced being suddenly thrust into a cultural or ethnic context that was foreign to us. Regardless of how well treated, we still felt we did not belong, did not fit in. Lack of strong alteregoing connections gives rise to a feeling of "having nothing in common," or to severe states of alienation. The depression that accompanies the cultural shock of moving from one ethnic environment to another has roots in the unavailability of alterego selfobjects (those whose psychological function it is to twin our own self's essential features). This need for alterego connections does not validate a segregationalist position of course. The central psychological issue being illustrated here is not the need for racial homogenity, but the state of narcissistic depletion which arises when one has limited or nil bonds with "like" selves.

Demands for twinship alteregoing were expressed by

one pastor who fumed about his wife and congregation: "I can't understand why they don't see things my way and respond as I do. It's perfectly clear. No one ever seems to look at situations from my perspective." Another pastor, whose alterego yearnings were not as intense, expressed great relief when he began to imagine that I, his alterego therapist, might have "crazy thoughts" at times, just as he did. Even more subtle was the quiet reassurance of normalcy and human connectedness when a significant person responded to a pastor's personal story with a simple but heartfelt, "I know what you mean."

In spite of clinical efforts to provide some discriminating marks between mirroring, idealizing, or alterego selfobject needs and responses, the distinction is not always clear. In the first place, even though the narcissistic classification gives us a degree of cognitive and emotional mastery, neither this classification or any other attempt to depict human reality can do full justice to the complexity of what it means to be a person. Furthermore, we have seen instances where narcissistic needs overlap or compensate for one another, even when one narcissistic configuration is central. Nonetheless, through clinical experience, personal introspection, and "thought experimentation,"[7] we can arrive at a fairly assured decision as to the nature of a self-selfobject relationship. Let us consider this episode.

An aged pastor from our congregation was confined to nursing-home care. Parkinson's disease had silenced his voice and much of his mind. On frequent occasions at the home, an elderly woman, who was disoriented and not responsible for her actions, would begin shrieking and screaming hysterically, with sedation the only effective intervention. To these turbulent outbursts the other residents would react with angry complaints, yelling at her to shut up. One day the enfeebled pastor was sitting next to her as she began her ritual wailing. After a few moments, his worn hand reached out and touched her gently on the arm—the way it had countless other arms in his ministry before, now perhaps in only an instinctual pastoral response, perhaps enabled by some breakthrough in his own clouded consciousness; but he touched her—and the disturbed woman became quiet and peaceful.

An immediate self-selfobject relationship had been established between these two aged individuals. A fragmenting, disharmonious self was made calm through the responsiveness of an empathic other self. But did the restoring function stem from a mirroring selfobject, an idealized selfobject, or an alterego selfobject? Although a reliable decision would necessitate a detailed examination of just what the two selves in this encounter were experiencing, it seems obvious that the elderly woman was not restored through mirroring affirmation of her self, nor through a soothing merger with the retired pastor as an idealized imago.

The woman was calmed through the presence of a human touch, through a humanizing touch, which conveyed in a primitive, beyond-words way that she was connected with humanity, linked with another human being who resonated with her anguish. She was not alone, for there was another of essential alikeness near her. The need of our selves for alterego responses, the need to experience that we are surrounded by others of like mind and manner, is as essential and powerful as our needs for mirroring and merger. Empathically, as well as through experience, we can come to discern the differences between these needs and thus, as available selfobjects for others, we can respond in sensitively appropriate ways. We consider, now, pastors whose lives and ministries reflect difficulties in this alterego sector of their selves.

I recall a female pastor who became angry at the apparent male-dominating language she heard me use during a presentation to convened ministers. As I listened atten-

tively to her in private, and as, in the warmth of this unexpected empathic response she spoke more personally,
she expressed hurt and frustration at not being accepted
by pastor colleagues as "one of the boys." I did not point
out her own unconscious use of a male-oriented figure of
speech in her effort to express a very real need within her
self. Language was not the problem. However she might
state it, she did not feel inwardly sustained by a comrade-
ship with ministering colleagues who, in her situation, were
primarily men. Although performing similar work and
proclaiming a similar gospel, these externals were not sufficient to provide deep within an abiding, supporting assurance of essential alikeness between herself and them.

She needed, in addition, the actual presence of colleagues, or the warm memories of those whom she experienced as her self, who understood her and were understood by her, with whom she could be in ministering
partnership as kindred spirits. Her problem was not rooted
in some gender dysphoria (dislike of her own femininity
or dislike of men), nor in personal identity crises. Her
problem was rooted in a legitimate narcissistic need, the
need to affirm her being and doing, and to know she belonged, via supporting alterego relationships. All of us require, throughout our life, a milieu of alterego support,
that largely nonverbal experience of sameness and identity
between our self and others which carries us through our
days not alone.

Women pastors may have special difficulties in finding
a satisfying alterego context. On the one hand, female pastors have had a history of being left out by male ministers
and marginally placed by their denominations. Regardless
of St. Paul's faith dictum that in the church as the body of
Christ there is neither male nor female, women ministers
have had to work hard to enter the male-dominated ranks
of the ordained clergy. In many cases, unfortunately, the
emotional alterego acceptance and embrace of women col-

leagues by male pastors and denominational leaders has lagged far behind. A cartoon in a journal for church leaders shows two male pastors obviously reminiscing about the good old days. One minister says to the other: "Remember back when we were young, and the difference between clergy and laity was none of the clergy were women?"[8] Obviously, the cartoonist recognized an ecclesiastical, and narcissistic, sore spot.

As a consequence of these narcissistic injuries to their selves, some women pastors become despondent. Commitment to parish work weakens, physical strength and enthusiasm ebb, ideals dim. Other women ministers, however, react with a good deal of narcissistic rage. One extremely capable woman with a gentle spirit confided to me after beginning her ministry with a chauvinistic senior pastor: "I never swore in my life. I only started to swear after I started working for him." Feeling isolated or patronized by unempathic male colleagues, women pastors also form their own exclusive professional associations. Such associations, formal and informal, can and do provide healthy alterego supports. At times, however, the focus of these associations centers on rageful reactions toward unreceptive males and male-dominated denominational structures.

Male pastors themselves, however, also struggle with the absence of alterego sustenance. Frequently, when pastors of both genders gather together for personal reflection, they speak sadly of "the loneliness of the ministry." As I listen to their stories, that loneliness appears to have two dimensions. On the one hand, ministers express a professional loneliness, being lonely in their *role* as pastor. Much like the women pastors, male ministers also feel cut off from a sense of being intimately connected with others like themselves. In particular, they work feeling isolated, or at worst alienated, from other pastors and from denominational leaders. Rev. David F.'s hypersensitivity may well have been ameliorated if the pastor of the large "successful" church had conveyed a spirit of colleagueship with the new man, empathically responding as one whom David F. could appropriate as a fellow sojourner in their common enterprise of ministry.

Another pastor related a typical situation where he offered his time and talents for whatever committee work the denomination might have, but never received a call, nor even acknowledgement of his offer from denominational staff. Gradually a bitter, distancing mood arose between himself and them. His effort to experience an alterego connection between himself and his work in the local parish, on the one hand, and the persons and work of the denomination, on the other, was thwarted. In place of a hopeful reaching out, the pastor withdrew, expressing to others his own forms of narcissistic rage.

Matters are frequently as frustrating within denominational staffs. One church official confided that he felt his talents and suggestions were "devalued" by other staff members, which caused him to withdraw in hurt and frustration. The injury here again arose not primarily as a blow to his grandiose self, nor as a rebuff from an idealized figure, but as an injury to his need for experiencing a unity with colleagues around common visions and shared functions. His commitment was to a "team ministry," in which even the leader would perform tasks all the rest were required to perform, in which *all* persons would mutually relieve and support one another.

His model of ministry (as well as his personal need) centered around the confirming, enlivening, responsibility-sharing interplay of alterego companions. Absence of such selfobject responsiveness ultimately lead him to leave denominational work. In spite of various programs instituted by denominations to overcome this sense of isolation and alienation of pastors from one another and from denominational leaders, the malady persists.

On the other hand, ministers also express a personal

loneliness, a feeling of isolation as a *person* in ministry. Older pastors relate how they have never been called by their first names by parishioners, even after long years of service within a congregation. Being addressed as "Dr. Jones," "Pastor," or "sir" may provide narcissistic gratification of grandiose-mirroring needs, but for some ministers it does not suffice for longed-after alterego familiarity.

Alterego injuries occur with young ministers as well. A recently ordained colleague told of the emotional reception given him when he entered the local bowling-alley bar: "When I came in, they all put their beer glasses down and became quiet. As I sat there, it became clear that they resented my crossing the boundary into their territory. I have never felt so isolated in all my life." Pastors hunger for personal relationships of unity and belonging with others they experience as like unto their selves. A pastor's self is made firm by the receptiveness and warmth of others whose moods, values, and styles comfortingly reflect, and thus confirm, the pastor's own.

For some ministers, the narcissistic injury of alterego isolation has been a chronic condition. Rev. John O. lost an eye when he was three. Largely as a consequence of this physical disability, which affected his depth perception and the development of his hand-eye coordination, he was often socially rejected. Nobody wanted him on their ball team. He was always chosen last when they had to let him play. He was the brunt of jokes. The pain of all this was bad enough without another torment: he didn't know why he wasn't like the other kids, why he couldn't hit the ball or catch it, why he sometimes stumbled when he ran.

Amazingly, his mother and father had in no way explained to him the normal consequences of his single sight. They had not conveyed to him how he would see things in a way different from the other kids, nor had they attempted to reassure him that the other kids were much like him, with their own problems and worries and uncertainties. Neither had they thought to help him foster friendships, by having children over to the house, for example. He was isolated, without playmates, without empathically supporting parents, and without an explanation. Consistent responses that treated him as an outsider resulted in a deeply sad belief that he was "a weird kid," who did not fit anywhere.

Before he turned nine, his family moved into an ethnic community where all the neighbors spoke a foreign language. Once again he was different, and once more left out. He spent his lonely days in private, obsessive activities where he tried to overcome his physical limitations. This only made the loneliness worse. It wasn't until his senior year that he found his first, tenuous friend.

John O.'s real handicap was not the loss of vision in one eye; the truly debilitating handicap was the traumatic loss of alterego others, those whose echoing-confirming responses could have grounded in his nuclear self the firm conviction of his normalcy, his belonging, and his humanity. His fragile self was alterego starved and vulnerable. Because he lacked these cohesion-producing alterego responses, he was never sure of himself. Obsessive activities of a physical and intellectual nature resulted in some private, grandiose satisfactions, but his developmentally thwarted self remained riveted on alterego needs.

"I've never been able to trust my own vision, either in terms of physical perception or emotional perception. For all the hurt, I still need other people as my lens. I need them to know if my vision is accurate. I not only get afraid when I think they are rejecting me, I also get afraid when I sense they are not seeing reality clearly, because then I'm afraid that I'll lose total touch with reality." Here is a tender witness to his and our essential need for alterego responses, without which we have neither a place in the world nor a hold on its reality.

Rev. John O.'s archaic but still developmentally appropriate need for alterego selfobjects motivated him to enter the ministry. Here there would be a community of sensitive individuals like himself, he conjectured, who would understand him and help him keep his perspectives clear. Here the mark of ordination would forever make him a member of that embracing fellowship of pastors, commonly called by God to serve. Unfortunately, however, his intense need for alterego responses quickly resulted in difficulties. His pastoral and administrative leadership was tentative. His preaching was dry and uninspiring. No one knew that before each meeting and before each Sunday morning he suffered repeated anxiety attacks, that from them he also became nauseated and cramped.

As he stood up to lead worship, he felt once more like that little one-eyed boy who was sure to be rejected. He couldn't help himself; the waves of foreboding flooded him, rendering him a washout. His ministry was dominated by the need for restoration of his vulnerable self through the alterego ministration of others. It did not happen. He had become a pastor for "social" reasons rather than "functional" reasons. "I wanted to 'belong,' but I realize now they expected me to 'serve,' to fulfill the functions, the role, of a pastor." His restoration fantasies of new life via ministry were finally demolished when the congregation, without speaking to him first or explaining why (shades of his flawed parental alteregos) made plans for his removal. He came to see me in a state of extreme depression, and not little rage. Clinically stated, his fragile self-cohesion was fragmenting in the face of narcissistic injuries sustained from the (for him) unempathic alterego parish.

Pastors are struggling. These struggles often center around narcissistic difficulties, where their self-cohesion is particularly vulnerable, weak, or defectively structured, and where their core needs and injuries are rooted in mirroring, idealizing, or alterego selfobject responses. We turn now to the selves of parishes. Our self psychology analysis will suggest that difficulties within parishes are based upon the same narcissistic struggles as found in pastors. It will be a short step, then, to Chapter 5, where the particular narcissistic need of the pastor meeting the particular narcissistic need of the parish gives rise to debilitating struggles between them.

Chapter 4

NARCISSISTIC STRUCTURES AND STRUGGLES OF PARISHES

A perceptive colleague tells of being dissuaded in seminary from writing a dissertation on "personalities of parishes." "You cannot apply individual psychology to complex, heterogeneous groups," warned his sociologically oriented professor. Methodology aside for the moment, just ask any minister. Ask if congregations have distinct "personalities" and you will see his face light up or grimace in affirmation. A conference minister who has placed scores of pastors in parish settings once mused: "It's very strange. You can completely change the cast of characters and still the church remains the same. It's like there are ghosts in the pews and pulpit."

Descriptions of parish personalities are not projected fantasies from the psyche of pastors. Neither are they positive or negative clusters of experience with significant individuals in a pastor's past now transferred onto a gathered body; i.e., the church is not "mother" writ large, for example. It is inaccurate to say, furthermore, that personality descriptions are anthropomorphizing efforts of ministers to transform that often confusing and overwhelming multiplicity called a church into "merely" an individual-type personality to be reckoned with. All of these may occur, of course, but the awareness that a congregation manifests persistent characteristics is based principally upon experience in and empathic observation of the lives of parishes themselves.

Self psychology supports these general insights. One of Kohut's important clinical contributions was to begin delineating how, through the method of empathic observation and introspection, a group can be understood to have a "self" analogous to the self of an individual. The self is formed and maintained, and its character given direction, via its central narcissistic needs, strengths, and selfobject respondents.[1] A group self like an individual self, needs empathic mirroring, idealizing, and alteregoing selfobject responses for the development and maintenance of its self-cohesion.

Group selves also developmentally unfold from archaic narcissistic states to mature ones, inevitably experience narcissistic injuries, tend to respond with some degree of withdrawal and/or rage to such injuries, and strive in mature or regressive ways to restore their fragmented cohesiveness and sense of well-being. Parishes have a "self," a group self. Those vicissitudes in self-cohesion, and those particular narcissistic orientations and characteristics we have encountered in the selves of pastors, occur in the selves of parishes as well. A parish's "personality" is a reflection of the character of its group self.

THE NATURE OF THE PARISH SELF

We need to make a clarification. We have been using the term "personality" in general to point to the persistent, underlying core of a parish, which self psychology has called the group self. In a strict sense, the self of a parish should not be considered the same as or equivalent to the personality of a parish, nor as the sum total of various personality "traits," just as the self of the individual should not be considered the same as or equivalent to the individual's "identity," nor as the integration of various "identities." The parish self grounds the parish's personality. The self as the center of the group's psychological world is the base upon which and by which a personality can be and is formed. This clarification is important here in order to distinguish between self-analysis and personality-analysis.

Personality typology systems used in self-study manuals for congregations focus on such traits as group size, leadership styles, patterns of communication, theological emphases, or social action orientations. These studies and the resulting church types they describe are often informative and helpful, but they fail to incorporate a depth-psychological understanding of the congregation's group self. Personality typologies do not touch the core of a parish's narcissistic makeup and struggles.

While I do not intend to provide anything close to a self-study manual for a church's self-appraisal, a broad, empathic grasp of the potential for healing or hurting that results from a solid or precariously formed self, and an empathic grasp of the narcissistic dynamics operative in the lives of all churches, can be means of grace for the restoration of parish and pastor alike.

Self-cohesion.   A central quality of the self of a parish or individual is the degree to which the self's structure is experienced as whole and continuous, fully alive and vigorous, balanced and organized, on the one hand; or, as riddled with defects, seriously enfeebled, disharmonious, on the other.[2] A spectrum of cohesiveness exists between these extremes of self-cohesion. Some congregations, unfortunately, exhibit chronically weak or inadequately structured parish selves. They typically have histories of unsuccessful relationships with pastors, are unable to keep new members or elicit involved participation from current members, are in conflict with one another or fail to be mutually supportive, show little enthusiasm for new programming, maintain a self-protecting status quo, tend to respond to difficult situations with despondency or outrage, seem unable to utilize the guidance or internalize the encouragement of helping professionals, and create a general atmosphere of aimlessness, rigidity, or anger around themselves.

The prognosis for these narcissistically disordered parishes is not hopeful. Symptoms of self-fragmentation or inadequate self-structure are varied, of course, and no symptom in itself is a sign of lost or defective self-cohesion. In each case, an empathic immersion into the life of the church is necessary in order to ascertain the health status of its self-cohesion and, as we shall discuss later, in order to grasp the nature of its narcissistic aims.

Other congregations whose developing self-cohesion has progressed fairly well may come to a juncture where their cohesiveness is in an immobilized, fixated state ("We're stagnating here! Just existing"), or where their self-cohesion is actually in a state of fragmentation ("Things are falling apart. Nothing works anymore."). The prognosis here is often more hopeful than in the case of seriously defective parish selves, inasmuch as these parishes tend to remain focused around vestiges of their healthily developed self-structure. In short, there is some effective and functioning nuclear core upon which to rebuild. As long as a religious community's self retains some degree of its former firmness, vitality, or functional organization, that community's beleaguered self-cohesion contains the potential for renewed movement toward development and fulfillment of its central projects and ideals.

Other parishes exhibit strong and adequately structured selves. They tend to be resilient in the face of threats to their nuclear goals, ideals, and sense of belonging. Narcissistic injuries do not decimate their sense of well-being, and empathy for one another and for others remains basically extended and operative, even when the parishes are struggling with economic, pastor, or parishioner problems. But *all* religious communities experience fluctuations in their self-cohesion from time to time, as many distressed congregations and clergy know. Just like individuals, parishes are inevitably vulnerable to some fragmentation of their self-cohesion, and thus given to some expression of narcissistic despondency and/or rage.

For all parishes, threats to established self-cohesion occur commonly when losses are experienced (of members, financial support, or community prestige, for instance), or when the parish is in a state of transition (from small to large, from one self-identity to another, or from old pastor to new). In both cases, the fabric of the parish self can be sorely tried.

I remember receiving a late evening call at home from a colleague I like and respect very much. His calm manner and gentle humor were disturbingly absent. They wanted him out, he said. After he had been there only a few short weeks, a small but vocal group in the new church he had come to serve were expressing disappointment in his ministry. Members who supported him told of the dissension being stirred up among church families. He was more crushed than angry, although the latter feeling was beginning to throb in his temples. His years at his previous church had been a blessing to its membership as well as to himself and his family. He had been a beloved pastor.

The expectation that this new flock, in his dreams *all* of these people, would receive him in the same way was shattered. He felt uncertain about himself. His stomach and chest were tight. He worried not only about his own career but about the well-being of this new congregation he had hoped to make his own. It was clear that he had suffered a narcissistic injury. As a result, the well-being of his self-cohesion was shaken. The parish, apparently, was also experiencing disruptions in its self-cohesion.

While such a disruption of a pastor or parish's self can arise any time, it commonly occurs in that transition period of weeks or years between old and new pastors. Certainly the pastors' personalities often play a significant part in all this, as do the theological, economic, social, and historical factors endogenous to the congregation. But the underlying psychological dynamic in these situations rests in the fact that whenever there are transitions in individual or corporate life, the prevailing cohesion of the person or group becomes tenuous.

Consider for a moment the dynamics operative when our children go into first grade or off to their first year of college. Their life structure changes. New expectations from their adult world, intensified pressures from peers, altered ways in how they will have to handle their body, their tears, their homesickness, all require them to give up or modify both their comfortable self-image and their fantasies of how the world is supposed to be for them. The cohesion of their self is shaken and vulnerable. Upset stomachs and bad dreams, increased irritation and regressive behavior, all attest to the fragmentation of their self-structure. It is something we expect to happen to a degree.

This shaking of internal structure happens to a congregation as well when it is in a transition stage, such as a change of pastors. A psychological vacuum is created in which those inner assurances, cherished ideas, and routine involvements that have held the group together in the past are to some degree endangered—in actuality or in worrisome anticipation. Unresolved but previously managed conflicts may reemerge disruptively as a result of the con-

gregation's jarred self-cohesion. Old hurts at being slighted
by previous pastor(s), denominational leaders, or even by
one another may cry anew for retribution. Suppressed
longings to assert power which others in the church acknowledge and bow to might openly flare. Talk of the
church "splitting," or anxious efforts to quell all dissension,
may materialize. The rise of anger and/or despair may
jeopardize the unique expressions of the congregation's
commitment and faith.

At such times, a church's less-than-nurturing responses
issue not from an insidious inner heart, but from a state
of lost narcissistic wholeness. That loss is hoped to prove
transitory. Typically it is. Much depends upon whether the
parish's nuclear self is firmly or precariously formed. That
self-cohesion, as we saw in the lives of pastors, arises from
the interaction between the parish's central narcissistic aims
and the more or less strength-producing responses of its
central selfobject figures.

Narcissistic orientations.   A congregation rarely, of course,
demonstrates a monochromatic personality. A variety of
viewpoints and goals expressed by divergent members
often marks the pluralistic quality of most religious communities. Central to what parishioners bring to this symbolic, selfobject place called "church" are their various narcissistic expectations and injuries. The way parishioners
structure their relationship with their church, therefore,
may be understood as a reflection of the state of their selves.[3]
Church structures, in turn, typically provide various selfobject opportunities for members' narcissistic enhancement
and restoration. Alterego selfobject needs may be met in
the contexts of community worship, youth fellowships, Bi-
ble-study groups, or social gatherings, where the sharing
of alikeness is celebrated and the sense of belonging fostered.

The need for nurturing via idealizing experiences may

be met through the inspiring presence of a pastor or priest, through worship which invokes the presence of God's comforting spirit, or by participation in uplifting values and purposes. Mirroring needs of parishioners may find appropriate avenues for expression and selfobject response through serving on church boards, ushering, or "letting your light so shine before men" through leading worship, evangelizing, or church-school teaching. Churches are narcissistically pluralistic, both in terms of parishioners' expectations and the numerous selfobject offerings provided by the church.

The reality of narcissistic variety does not mean that all narcissistic orientations are psychologically equal in the self of a parish, or that the parish self has no nuclear narcissistic configuration around which it is primarily formed, and by which it is maintained via appropriate selfobject responses. Empathic observation of congregational life tends to indicate that the parish self, like the individual self, congeals around a particular primary or compensatory narcissistic orientation.[4] While perhaps exhibiting dimensions of all three narcissistic aims (mirroring, idealizing, alteregoing), and while there may be competing/conflicting narcissistic aims among parishioners, there tends to be one narcissistic disposition that remains centrally dominant in the parish.

The narcissistic orientation of a parish may change from time to time, however. A congregation striving to fulfill its primary narcissistic need may move to a reliance upon a compensating selfobject response when that primary narcissistic aim is thwarted in some way. For example, a congregation motivated by the grandiose-mirroring sector of its self was forced to face the embarrassment of public scandal and denominational intervention when their much acclaimed pastor was caught shoplifting. The congregation, in an effort to soothe itself and regain its sense of well-being (self-cohesion), withdrew into an idealizing merger with God. The boundaries of the church temporarily shrank to where worship, prayer, confession, and reliance upon God's divine guidance and care characterized their self's spirit.

Another congregation, rocked by the disclosure of an idealized pastor's extramarital affair, moved to an alter-egoing embracing of one another as means of narcissistic restitution. In cases such as these, the compensating narcissistic aims may give a certain cast to the parishes' future. Typically, however, a parish will move back again to its primary narcissistic aim when its narcissistic equilibrium is reestablished.

More permanent alterations of a church's narcissistic orientation also occur. This process is commonly set in motion when a congregation's neighborhood changes, and thus the character of its membership. Rapid industrial development in a semirural area resulted in unexpected church growth for one small congregation. Within a few years, the budget increased, the range and type of programs changed, new parishioners became major lay leaders, and a pastor with strong administrative abilities was called. Those individuals who had literally built the church nail by plank, who had expected its walls to remain comfortably familiar, quickly found their ecclesiastical haven invaded by "those people." The strong alterego orientation of the small congregation was steadily replaced by a growing grandiose-mirroring attitude, as new members and the pastor envisioned the church as the community's guiding and shining light. As might be expected, intense conflict arose between those who felt disenfranchised and those who saw themselves as the new majority.

The core narcissistic aim of a parish self may be very obvious. On the other hand, it may be difficult to discern, and the shifts in a congregation's narcissistic orientation may be slow and nearly imperceptible. In any case, the "personality" of a parish is shaped in large measure by the

quality of its self-cohesion and the character of its grandiose-mirroring, idealization-merger, or alterego core.

Consequently, neither a diversity of parishioner personalities within a congregation, nor a uniformity of personalities, should be taken as the central dynamics determining or expressing the nature of the communal self.
Similarly, neither the existence of congregational conflict,
nor the fact of congregational unanimity, should be considered the primary determiners or expressions of the
presence, absence, or character of bonding within the parish. Instead, the presence, absence, or character of psychological bonding within the parish self reflect its particular narcissistic core.

A psychosocial diagnosis of a congregation as "conflictual" or "cooperative," for example, fails to realize that
the very nature of the "conflict" or "cooperation" stands
in need of a deeper, self psychological interpretation. Congregational conflict may represent severe disintegration of
the parish self—spiritually, socially, or economically—due
to the loss of an idealized, cohesion-maintaining pastor.

Or, congregational conflict may represent a regressive
type of group unity, wherein anger and noisy discord are
the means for maintaining some sense of grandiose power,
vitality, or semblance of intactness. Then again, congregational conflict may represent a healthy and expected
means for hammering out decisions among alterego parishioner selves, who harbor minimal feelings of mortification (narcissistic injuries) and minimal fantasies for revenge (narcissistic rage).

Congregational cooperation, for its part, may represent the cohabitation of incongruous members welded together pragmatically by fanatical desires for mirroring
glorification. Or, congregational cooperation may represent a surrender of parishioners' selves to the overarching
will of an idealized religious cult leader. Then again, congregational cooperation may exist as a result of a communal

self flexibly and harmoniously working out its own ideal values of service and caring.

A parish self comes into existence, and is maintained, as diverse persons are united by core narcissistic aims and selfobject influences, which lie beneath and give shape to those theological, ethical, social, and political activities and goals publicly declared and followed. Each church is psychologically animated by the unique character of its narcissistic makeup.

We now address ourselves more specifically to how the congregational self is formed and maintained.

FORMATION AND MAINTENANCE OF THE PARISH SELF

The development of a parish self is a complex process. Whatever the theological, sociological, or political factors involved, at work psychologically in the formation and maintenance of every communal self is the mobilization and organization of particular narcissistic needs of individuals (parishioners) through the galvanizing power or representative presence of selfobject leaders (in particular, pastors). Sometimes the selfobject pastor is dominant in giving a congregation its corporate life and narcissistic cast.

At other times, a congregation's self is shaped and maintained more by the pressing demand of its own inherent narcissistic strivings, with only secondary concern about the personhood of its pastoral selfobject respondent or representative. A spectrum of varying mixtures of group-self needs and selfobject influences exists. But always, for a group as well as for an individual, the self-selfobject connection is inseparable. That is, the narcissistic orientation of the parish self is inseparable from the milieu of its selfobjects, in particular the pastor as the crucial selfobject figure.

In this complex process of communal self-formation and maintenance, not only do pastors become selfobjects for parishes, but parishes often become selfobjects for pastors. On the healthy side, this can increase self-esteem in both, and thus enhance the capacity for empathic responses to others. At times, however, the hyperstimulation of mutual idealization and admiration can result in the selves of a parish and a pastor expanding beyond the confines of their physical and intellectual limitations, where they move toward archaic beliefs in the invincibility of their strength and the inerrancy of their truth.

At other times, when each may experience the devastation of selfobject rejection and failure, the psychological state of their selves may shrink. When this occurs, the only semblance of a remaining parish self may be contained in a single one of its group functions (worship as the sole occasion for communal participation, for example), or group aims (a preoccupation with meeting the church's mortgage payment, for instance), or group actions (such as keeping alive the church's food pantry).[5] In the analysis to follow, the complex relationship of communal selfobjects and core narcissistic needs of the parish self are dealt with separately only for the purpose of deeper understanding and interpretation.

Selfobject pastors.   The parish self does have selfobject figures other than their pastors. The nuclear core of the parish self may reside in or be carried by just a few influential members. A congregation may congeal around a number of parishioners who, although not the majority, initiate action and provide rationale which others follow. These influential few function as selfobject figures whose thoughts and style shape the mentality and ministry of a congregation.

The narcissistic bonding of a congregation, however, often centers principally around a selfobject pastor. To begin with, a parish self may be formed and/or maintained around a commanding, persuasive, or charismatic pastor by whose grandeur the religious community can feel assured of continued high self-esteem and well-being. Clinically stated, a pastor whose style and approach is animated primarily by the grandiose-mirroring sector of his self may focus parishioners' own narcissistic needs for grandiose-mirroring recognition.[6] The grandiose dimensions of the pastor's self mobilizes grandiose-mirroring hopes, fantasies, or behavior in the parish's own self. The narcissistic orientation and bonding of the parish, therefore, takes its direction principally from the influence of the pastor's grandiose self.

In many instances this narcissistic configuration is quite obvious. We all know congregations that have been structured around culturally recognized pastors famous for their preaching prowess, or around pastors whose powerful and expansive personalities forge remarkable church growth and social prominence. It is common in these situations to hear parishioners brag about how wonderful their minister is and what they as a church have accomplished, all said with a tone of personal pride, if not superiority. The self-certainty and charisma of the selfobject pastor tends to stimulate similar feelings of narcissistic assuredness, if not omnipotence, within the congregation.

Other congregations whose cohesiveness emanates primarily from a healthily assertive pastor are not as narcissistically expansive, and neither are the manifestations of their pastor's grandiose self. Such parishes exhibit a quieter pride in themselves, their ministers, and their service, and are sustained in esteem by appreciations from a smaller circle of community and denominational figures. While less obvious than the ostensible congregations, these parish selves are also formed and/or maintained around pastoral leaders whose style, attitudes, and beliefs are connected primarily with the grandiose sectors of their selves.

While elements of idealization may be involved in all of these instances, the narcissistic bonding here consists of parishes' *identification* with an omnipotent selfobject pastor, rather than their *merger* with an idealized selfobject pastor.[7] Via this identification, a parish's own grandiose self is enhanced, focused, or released from repression. The dynamic, simply put, is not so much "He is great and we are great because we are part of him," but "He is great and makes us feel great, too."

A pastor who fosters pride and healthy self-esteem in the parish by word or example can be a faithful servant. The needs of the individual and group for mirroring acclaim are normal and necessary. With some consideration for the "optimal frustration" of these needs in their passage from immature to mature forms, a pastor's enhancement of the parish's grandiose self can contribute to firm and reliable self-cohesion in the parish, even when the pastor leaves.[8]

Some congregations in the midst of declining enrollment, for example, retain a high opinion of themselves and their histories through the cherished memory of having been served by theologically renowned pastors. The ego-enhancing messages sounded in hundreds of sermons and pastoral newsletters can lodge firmly in the heart of a religious community, keeping it vibrant and hopeful even in the wake of environmental change or decay. Perhaps even the disciples, as the core of the early church, were sustained in their ministry by a glow of healthy grandiosity, infused in them by their commission from the resurrected Christ (Matt. 28:18–20).

The narcissistic bonding of a parish self via identification with a charismatic or commanding selfobject pastor can, however, be archaic in nature and ultimately destructive. The aura of a pastor's authority may lead to entrenched programs and policies, where opposing points of view are stifled if not sharply rebuked, and where the spiritual or administrative efforts of successive pastors are thwarted by the church, or critically compared to the predecessor's. The archaically structured parish self may move to a paranoidlike effort to protect its power and prestige. Excessive grandiosity in a religious body can exclude empathic sensitivity toward others, and result in rigid beliefs and doctrines.

Rather than being the grandiose selfobject figure with which to identify, the narcissistically imbued clergy may serve as the *bearer* or *representative* of the grandiose-mirroring wishes of others. For example, in their search for a pastor, a congregation with a healthy or elevated sense of its own importance will scrutinize all candidates in an effort to locate one who can sufficiently represent and further their own narcissism. Not only will the candidate's theological orientation or preaching ability become decisive factors in the selection process, but so will his physical looks, clothing style, cultural background, and spouse's demeanor. Candidates, of course, never read this in the job description, and rarely hear of it in the interview, due in large part to that fact that this wish and need for a narcissistic representative is often disavowed if not repressed by the congregational body.

Such is not always the case, however. One colleague tells of a search committee from a haughty congregation feeling extremely insulted when, after bestowing upon him the honor of selection, their new pastor replied that he first had some questions about them before deciding whether they were the kind of a congregation he would like to serve. In any case, a candidate who is not aware of the parish's narcissistic freight, which he is expected to carry, has trouble in store, as we shall see in the next chapter.

Archaic and destructive forms of this narcissistic alliance, where the leader represents and carries the grandiose-mirroring needs and expectations of the group, also exist. As a secular example, which Kohut often cited, Hitler's genocidal demands for retribution for his personally injured narcissistic self—individual and cultural rebuffs to his narcissistic needs for public acclaim—drew to him those others who, personally and as a nation, had suffered narcissistic injuries through some form of disenfranchisement. The grandiose promises and actions of Hitler galvanized a nation who found in him that selfobject representative through whom narcissistic retributions and reempowerment of their own grandiose selves would be obtained.[9]

Similarly, religious communities enraged over injustices done them are vulnerable to impulsive mobilizations around a chosen pastor whom they anticipate will carry forward the battle against malicious interlopers and reestablish a right order. In this narcissistic state, congregations, just like secular groups, at times unfortunately embrace external forces which they self-deceptively proclaim as justified actions based on ideals and values, when in reality the actions and system of supposed values express the parish self's narcissistic rage and social regression.

In the Award-winning movie, *Places in the Heart,* the community murder of the naive black youth, after he accidentally shot the town sheriff, represents the rise of whites' narcissistic rage over this insult to their superiority, and the seductive use of violent force wrested into a righteous instrument of social values and justice. Not even the highly principled and deeply religious widow protested the murder and public humiliation of the boy's body. It was what had to be done. Similarly, the actions of religious bodies undertaken for "righteous indignation," "salvation" or "humanitarian" reasons can fill volumes with their horror. Any sense of victory by such a religious group seems to confirm the grandiosity of their communal self.

Other narcissistic configurations exist besides the grandiose-mirroring orientation. A congregation may congeal around a pastor whose style and approach emanate primarily from the idealization sector of his self. Individuals thereby may be drawn into community by this selfobject figure *whose own self* is given up to an idealized value, vision, or virtue. The inspiring image of this person wedded to and embodying that higher truth or divine purpose attracts persons whose selves are oriented toward, or in desperate need of, merger with an idealized figure.

Here the selfobject pastor is the target for the idealizing needs and wishes of cohesively firm parishioners who find their selves uplifted, supported, and spiritually nurtured by being in resonating contact with the revered pastor. Here the selfobject pastor is also the target for the idealizing needs and longings of parishioners whose self-cohesion is weak, enfeebled, or fragmentation-prone. In the idealization relationship, parishioners psychologically *merge* with the selfobject pastor, thus becoming reassuringly calmed, soothed, and empowered by the pastor's wisdom, peacefulness, or perfection.

While grandiose elements were a part of Mahatma Gandhi's narcissism, at the core of his self-structure was a mystical merger with transcendent values expressed in concretely social, economic, and political forms. His nuclear self was driven by the need to express and fulfill those visionary ideals for humankind, rather than by personal mirroring motivations or even alterego yearnings. Gandhi riveted together a warring, factious India via his spirit-inspiring, to-the-death devotion to ultimate principles of life which, in his physical frailty and the power of his will, he wondrously embodied. In this consummate incarnation of transcendent values, he mobilized deep religious and social sensitivities in combative groups and individuals, lifted these selves beyond themselves into realms of supreme purpose and direction, and became the nation's cultural-spiritual selfobject rallying point.

Most of us pastors are not Gandhis, but often we are Ghandi-like. Parish selves are often bound narcissistically via some degree of idealization of their minister. A worshipful respect for God, or a sense of being divinely guided and cared for, are often spiritually prefaced by a relationship with an idealized pastor of great devotion and faith. Likewise, psycho-spiritual merger with God's grace and peace is mediated by pastors who serve as our spiritual fathers or mothers. Pastors who empathically allow such idealization of themselves, rather than discourage or deny such efforts, assist thereby in the development of parishioner and parish self-cohesion.

This narcissistic bonding can, of course, be archaic and ultimately destructive. One congregation's idealization of their pastor emeritus was so complete that emotionally they could not allow anyone to take his place. Even when the skill of the new minister finally made him "professionally acceptable," he still found there was no place for him in the community. Similar, but carried to the last degree, is the wide spectrum of individuals who made up Jonesville. Here idealizing prone or starved selves were united in a group merger with Rev. Jim Jones who offered himself as their earthly deity. Even for those few who realized his pathology, their own longings for nearness to such an idealized, messianic figure eclipsed their perception. This same attraction and surrender to idealized, powerful figures also operates in the main with those followers of Rev. Sun Yung Moon and similarly formed cults.

Rather than being the explicit, idealized selfobject with which to merge, an idealized pastor can also serve as the bearer or representative of the ideals of others, thus forming and/or maintaining a community self around these seminal values. Selfobject power still accrues to the pastoral leader, however, inasmuch as he personifies and perpetuates the group's ideological core. Jerry Falwell of the Moral Majority, for example, is an articulate, TV-attractive selfobject representative for that group of religious individuals whose ideals and espoused way of life are being sorely tried by Western culture and mores. Any serious discrepancy, however, between Falwell's ideology and that of the beleaguered-now-besieging Moral Majority group could well result in his rapid decline in the eyes of many present admirers. Failure of idealized selfobjects to carry and represent the group's central tenets often triggers the group's narcissistic rage, and, as the Bible says, "great is the fall of them."

The expectation that a pastor will personify and represent the idealized values, programs, and policies of a parish is a more theologically and culturally acceptable narcissistic expectation. Thus while a candidate for a pastoral position may well not be asked if she or he has what it takes to enhance the congregation's social prominence and prestige (this pride being theologically considered "sinful," and culturally considered "egotistical"), the candidate will surely be expected to demonstrate his or her inclination and ability to further the ideological standards and goals of the religious body (such ideals being conceived as "Christian" or "loving").

Finally, while parish selves are not typically formed around alterego pastors, they are maintained and served by alterego selfobject leaders. There are religious communities "called together" by the commonness of their spirit and theology, in which the pastor functions as the organizing alterego agent in this "priesthood of all believers." One congregation I worked with laughed heartily when I explained the idealizing-merger and grandiose-mirroring orientations, and asked them if they experienced their pastor as one they would feel inclined to be part of (merger) or to be strongly lead by (mirroring). "Neither," they said, "Bill is just one of us, working toward the goals we all have in common. We are all on the same level under the Lordship of Christ. Bill might *wish* that we idealized him more, though!" The good-natured humor of this strong congregation indicated an affection and appreciation for their pastor; but his functions and role were not considered something that set him apart from them. Alterego bonding tended to characterize much of this parish's self.

In similar fashion, much that transpires in "house churches" is of an alterego nature. The "leader," who is often a member of the clergy, leads not through the power of his grandiose or idealized self, but through the power of alterego self-exposure. The leader generates trust and helps create a caring climate by exposing his story and struggles, thereby inviting others to know themselves as human, and to experience new depths of human belonging.

It is normal and natural for people to seek out people like themselves in churches. Historically, in American experience, denominations and parishes have emerged along linguistic, racial, economic, and cultural lines. Parishes, therefore, have tended to become alterego homogeneous institutions. In some cases, where the church becomes the preserver and nurturer of special traditions and subcultures, this alterego relating may become the parish's primary reason for being. If the parish's cohesion is threatened, or if the parish self is fixated in archaic, unmodified alterego states, the parish may fiercely protect its ethnicity or identity from all invaders, making unwelcome those who are or seem to be "different." If by force of circumstance new members do enter and assert their "different" orientations, then narcissistic tensions arise. "Cold wars" are then waged among parishioners, the pastor is often blamed, and people may leave. The more rigid the narcissistic demand, the more vulnerable the parish is to narcissistic injuries and fragmentation.

Core narcissistic needs.   As stated previously, a parish self is psychologically structured by its dominant mirroring, idealizing, or alterego need, and by the availability and quality of its selfobject figures. We have just examined the complex narcissistic relationships a parish may establish with its selfobjects, particularly with pastors. We now consider in more isolated fashion the parish's core narcissistic orientation. These narcissistic orientations may be archaic in nature, with the particular church exhibiting subtle to blatant demands that others respond to it as the church deems its proper and rightful due.

Rageful reactions and/or feelings of depletion can result when the parish realizes that others are failing to accept its faith stance or social action (blows to the church's grandiose-mirroring needs); or when the church's leaders "fall from the way"—from the idealized embodiment of values and purposes the church upholds (blows to the church's need for merger with idealized figures). This can also be the case when the congregation experiences that supposedly like-minded others, who are counted on to support the fellowship with their kindred spirit, physical companionship, and steady dollars, have failed to make their echoing presence and presents available (blows to the church's need for alterego responses).

We consider briefly now vignettes that highlight the centrality of alterego, idealization, and mirroring needs in parishes.

St. J.'s began as a fledgling congregation meeting in a school gymnasium. Quickly that small group became enthusiastic over plans for erecting its own church building. For over 2 years these nuclear members pledged together their monies, immersed themselves in one another socially, and labored side by side on the new church until its completion. Reconstruction of the history of this congregation suggested that cohesion was basically established, and a group self formed, through strong needs for alterego connections. The nuclear members showed little interest in receiving public recognition, either from the community or the denomination (mirroring needs were low). While they professed a faith, they did not seem inspired by towering religious beliefs they strove to fulfill (idealizing inclinations were minimal).

Instead, this particular configuration of members longed for a reassuring sense of belonging, where the dedication and perspective of others matched, and thereby enhanced, their own. This core need was reinforced generally by a climate of anomie in their town, and reinforced specifically by the life-cycle need of many new members who were also new parents seeking a place for companionship and mutual support. Helping to solidify this orientation was the church's first pastor who, from his liberal point of view, proclaimed that anything they believed was acceptable, and who, from his own needs for alterego connections, promoted the social structuring of the congregation. St. J.'s alteregoing orientation was expressed through the persistent image they used to describe their self: "We are a family."

The building project provided that occasion wherein intense alterego relating could flourish and alterego needs could be met. The pervasive need for an alterego environment generated enthusiasm for the building project and lead to the cooperative efforts of these alterego hungry members. Throughout the ongoing life of this congregation, forms of worship, calendars of social activities, decision-making processes, and expectations of how the pastor was to conduct his ministry and where he was to live, were shaped by this underlying alterego orientation.

Later, however, after the church was built, the excitement wore off, the pastor left, and the financial grind of meeting mortgage payments set in, the alterego solidarity of the parish began to crumble. "Fun" social events became, of necessity, fund-raising events. Unrest caused some members to leave, which made meeting the church budget more difficult, which set in motion a mood of gloom and a self-perpetuating spiral of disintegration. At one point the parish came within a signature's breath of selling their church to a commercial firm.

Members who recalled those early, blissful days yearned for a return to them. The only problem was, there was nothing substantial to return to. There was no church other than an assembly of alterego relating. Nonetheless, St. J.'s wanted their new, second pastor to reestablish "the family atmosphere." He, instead, wanted to establish a core of worship and service that had a sustained and integral life of its own, where alterego involvements would be possible but not primary. It became clear that the fragmentation of this parish self was rooted in difficulties in its overextended alterego core.

Difficulties also arise from archaically based alterego orientations. Religious groups that demand uniformity of thought and belief, if not of behavior and dress, can elicit considerable devotion, for a member is surrounded by others who constantly twin the member's self, who in turn twin the other members. The reinforced self-perceptions, by the multireflections of self by alterego others, can give the individual and the religious body an elevated sense of superiority which looks down at those who are "not like us." Furthermore, strong alterego attachments often accompany devotion to an idealized leader, which can also intensify the bonding within the group. The cohesiveness of the group self, formed by alterego relating and amplified by narcissistic attachments to a selfobject figure, can result in a religious community of staggering institutional power, and remarkable insensitivity to outsiders.

We encounter a more inspiring example of congregational life when considering St. M.'s, a parish formed and maintained around the idealization sector of its self. From the outset, St. M.'s appeared to be a prime candidate for dissension and unrest, inasmuch as it was a hybrid merger of two well-established congregations, having different denominational backgrounds and diverse interests, moving into only one of the two church buildings. Moreover, different stories abounded as to why the merger came to be in the first place. But, remarkably, there were few ecclesiastical headaches.

Each party had come into the merger with a strong

self-image and solid self-esteem. Neither had to sublimate its self to a dominant other. Having been located in the same community, there were sufficient alterego links to overcome the alterego dissimilarities. The new parish also exhibited healthy grandiosity in being ready to spend several thousands of dollars on a new organ, and remodeling.

But more crucial than this, St. M.'s was welded together by a intense commitment to idealized values and purposes. Its central aim and design was to care for people beyond its self, to be a "world-outreach church," to fulfill Christ's command to bind up the broken-hearted. And it did so in astonishingly wide, complete, and creative ways. Although members lobbied for their own programs and expressed dislike for others proposed, parishioners felt themselves united in the larger project of world service. In a genuine way this congregation manifested one of the highest forms of narcissistic development, namely the capacity for "cosmic narcissism," that is, the capacity to feel empathically connected with and concerned for the whole world.[10] The parish's idealizing core gave it a vitality that was truly a blessing to others as well as to its self.

Others parishes bonded around idealization cores are not always as gracious. One congregation whose "specialty," as they called it, was "commitment to being Christ in the world," was filled with self-starting parishioners. This high-energy parish had no room for anyone who couldn't match their enthusiasm or commitment to this central mission. More extreme are religious bodies who demand rigid adherence to confessed principles, and who publicly chastise members caught in sinful violation. Not infrequently, these cases become media news stories.

Finally, we encountered the centrality of archaic grandiose-mirroring needs in the "second-best" congregation described in the Introduction. Chronic hypersensitivity to narcissistic injuries, an accumulation of narcissistic tensions through the years, and the lack of strong ministerial leadership—all these eroded efforts for stabilization, and left the parish operating from a regressive state of feeling and fantasy. Although emotionally vulnerable and resource-limited, the parish continued to seek narcissistic restoration through the empowering responses of community recognition and acclaim. Its repeated failures increased its despair and rage, as well as the persistence of its narcissistic aim. Whether that core narcissistic orientation was primary, regressively compensatory and transient, or permanently compensatory, is uncertain. In any case, the state of archaic demands for mirroring responses was clearly cardinal.

Years upon years of energy can be expended by a church in an effort to have its pressing, unsatisfied, and unmodified narcissistic needs met. Years upon years of energy can also be expended in an effort to overcome wrongs done to it. Church bodies not infrequently hold on to slights they have suffered from a pastor or from a group of parishioners decades ago. These real or imagined insults linger in the collective memory of the church's self, demanding justice, and detracting from the possibilities for newly developed self-cohesion.

Less intense, but still as persistently structured around a grandiose-mirroring orientation, is St. T.'s who, as one parish-sensitive observer stated, "Really thinks it is *it*." St. T.'s never saw itself as a part of a larger whole, whether that whole was the denomination to which it belonged in name only, or the community in which it was located. In defining itself as "a quality church," all furnishings had to be extremely fine, and anything that needed to be done was always an "in-house" project, with no outside contracting. Whatever institution it deemed necessary for itself, such as a retirement home, it constructed for itself. Enormous endowments gave it a feeling of invulnerability, which allowed it to continue in its insular, noncollaborative ways. For decades, a pattern had been established where the associate pastor eventually became the senior pastor, even though an official search was made. Continuity and exclusiveness were thereby insured.

The congregation now finds itself being challenged by a changing neighborhood and by the influx of a new type of parishioner—the Yuppies—the young, urban, professionals. These individuals are looking for more democratic involvement, for different pastoral leadership, and for more social consciousness on the part of St. T.'s. An intense, internal narcissistic struggle is underway in the congregation for the first time in its 100-year history. St. T.'s assumed and historically exhibited grandiose self is being threatened. As a result, powerful forces are being set in motion to preserve its special personality. New countervailing forces are also being mobilized. St. T.'s narrow narcissistic orientation may now be its undoing.

What provides the psychological bonding of a church, forming it into a group self and giving it its "personality," is the character of its underlying narcissistic orientation and the quality of its self-cohesion. The narcissistic structure of the parish self, guiding the nature of its action and giving rise to its assessed feeling of well-being, helps us understand why a congregation that appears financially successful, and without pastoral leadership problems or internal conflict, may still be listless in spirit, lack joy in worship, and react perfunctorily in its service to others; while a congregation struggling financially, or dealing with difficult consequences of a changing neighborhood, may still feel an intense aliveness, sense God's guiding intentions in all it endures, and respond compassionately toward strangers. One begins to grasp the nature of the pastor's self and the parish's self when empathically observing and understanding their underlying narcissistic structures and struggles.

Chapter 5

PATTERNS OF NARCISSISTIC STRUGGLE BETWEEN PASTORS AND PARISHES

Pastors and parishes long to feel whole and secure. Their selves reach out for responses that confirm that they are admired, immersed in the specialness of significant figures, and surrounded by like-spirited others. When pastors and parishes meet, they stimulate these narcissistic hopes and repressed wishes in each other. At the same time, all the self-difficulties in each become spontaneously mobilized as selfobject expectations and demands.

On the one hand, therefore, opportunities arise for restoration of weak or disordered selves; on the other hand, potent possibilities exist for re-injured self-esteem, fragmentation of self-cohesion, and the rise of narcissistic rage or withdrawal. When the latter occurs, pastors and parishes will struggle to maintain a tenuous and primitive psychological organization, at whatever cost. This chapter is about those struggles as they arise in that ecclesiastical interface between the pressing narcissistic needs of pastors and the pressing narcissistic needs of parishes.

Patterns of these narcissistic struggles can be described by correlating the various selfobject needs of each. The following diagram indicates the nine basic narcissistic configurations that can arise between pastor and parish when their dominant selfobject hope/expectation/demand is taken as the psychologically organizing principle. These configurations are not artificially generated. On the one hand, they are based on the living data of selves' narcissistic requirements and inclinations. On the other hand, they are "experience-near," as Kohut would put it; that is, pastors and parishioners can readily recognize and identify with the various patterns of involvement.

These nine configurations are not to be construed as an ecclesiastical typology. In the first place, each config-

Narcissistic Configurations

	CHURCH'S NEED TO IDEALIZE PASTOR	CHURCH'S NEED TO BE MIRRORED BY PASTOR	CHURCH'S NEED FOR ALTEREGO PASTOR
PASTOR'S NEED TO IDEALIZE	"A" Idealization-Merger as Mutual Need of Parish and Pastor	"D" Mirroring Needs of Parish Meet Idealization Needs of Pastor	"G" Alterego Needs of Parish Meet Idealization Needs of Pastor
PASTOR'S NEED TO BE MIRRORED	"B" Idealization Needs of Parish Meet Mirroring Needs of Pastor	"E" Grandiose-Mirroring as Mutual Needs of Parish and Pastor	"H" Alterego Needs of Parish Meet Mirroring Needs of Pastor
PASTOR'S NEED FOR ALTEREGO RELATING	"C" Idealization Needs of Parish Meet Alterego Needs of Pastor	"F" Mirroring Needs of Parish Meet Alterego Needs of Pastor	"I" Alterego Relating as Mutual Need of Parish and Pastor

Figure 5-1   Narcissistic Configurations

uration may be expressed in a variety of ways, and with varying degrees of intensity. Second, while certain narcissistic orientations become dominant, the self of a parish or pastor is shaped and guided by all three selfobject needs. Once again I attempt to provide a psychological framework, a perspective from which the vast expressions and levels of narcissistic relating can begin to be discerned with some depth and clarity. We are dealing here with "patterns." No church can be summarily categorized via one of these narcissistic configurations; but every church and every pastor can broaden their understanding of their own self and the self of the other by introspective reflection guided by these descriptions of narcissistic relationships.

"A": MUTUAL IDEALIZATION NEEDS

In this narcissistic configuration, both the pastor and the parish search for idealized selfobject figures with whose power, ideals, or wisdom they can merge for the strengthening of their own selves. The idealizing-inclined or hungry pastor looks for the parish to function in self-soothing and reassuring ways. The parish, in turn, borrows the values and strengths carried by the idealized selfobject pastor for the maintenance of its own self-cohesion. The more a self lacks inner balancing capacities and strong guiding ideals necessary for firm self-cohesion, the more dependent that self is upon idealized selfobject responses.

A pastor who relies heavily upon the self-cohesion maintaining responses of idealized figures will be disinclined to allow himself to be idealized, or will be unable to present himself as an adequate target for idealization. The idealizing-prone parish, unable to maintaining its own harmony and motivation, is, in turn, ill-equipped to care for the pastor's narcissistic needs. The general result in this instance is a devitalized, leaderless church. Neither the self of the pastor nor the self of the parish is able on its own to generate sustained enthusiasm for its goals and projects, nor are they supported and directed by their own internalized values and meanings. Each looks to the other to fulfill this function, only to find one's emptiness in the face of the hoped-for selfobject.

In one case, where the pastor relied upon the church council for direction and guidance, while the council's floundering self required shoring up by a confident, inspiring pastor, the pastor's wife began to provide the life-sustaining leadership that neither clergy or congregation could muster.

If we consider the concrete issue of the pastor's financial compensation from this configuration of mutual idealization-merger needs, we see the foundation of a common but frustrated fantasy. The pastor's idealizing tendencies may incline him to focus on the congregation as the "people of God." Whether articulated or not, the pastor anticipates being embraced by the idealized caring and nurturing congregation (a selfobject replacement for failed or absent parental selfobjects).

In particular, the pastor's narcissistic expectation is that his financial needs will be optimally considered and met by the God-loving and people-sensitive parish. Images of economic security provided by the congregation's numbers, financial resources, and idealized thoughtfulness are quietly harbored. Such narcissistic fantasies may be shaken when the pastor encounters a congregation who expects to be led by an idealized "suffering servant" who, in dedication and commitment to higher spiritual values, is not seriously concerned with money and is free from striving after mammon. The pastor's *giving* of self rather than *receiving* is taken by the parish as the essential nature and role of its idealized leader.

Eventually the structurally weak pastor and parish become disillusioned with each other. If narcissistic disap-

pointments are intense, and the selves of each are not sho-
red up by compensating selfobject responses (mirroring or
alterego), both pastor and parish may lapse into a state of
depressive withdrawal and lifelessness. Here the pastor
mechanically performs only the minimum of his ministering duties. Here church functions are sparsely attended,
and church committees fail to convene. Sunday morning
visitors quickly sense the lack of spiritual and emotional
vitality.

Forms of narcissistic rage may also be expressed by
the church, either in a passive way, such as coldness toward
the pastor, or failing to repair the parsonage, or in an active
way, such as giving the pastor an ultimatum. The pastor
may also respond with de-idealizing rage, angrily contemplating a move to a "good" parish, or a move outside the
ministry altogether. Unfortunately, in the placement system of most denominations, weak churches tend to be
wedded with weak pastors, resulting in further narcissistic
injury to and self-depletion of parish and pastor.

"B": IDEALIZING PARISH—GRANDIOSE PASTOR

The most traditional and familiar narcissistic configuration between pastor and parish is that in which the congregation seeks an idealized selfobject pastor, and the pastor looks for a congregation to mirror his grandiose self
(historically, even up to the present time, that pastoral figure has typically been male). During a service celebrating
a church's hundredth anniversary, a former pastor stated
to the gathered congregation that he did not consider it
appropriate for parishioners to call him by his first name.
He was to be formally addressed, for God had given him
a special responsibility in the church. He had been "set
apart" from others for this "awesome task" of seeing to
people's salvation, and that role required others to respond
to him with the recognition due his office.

In certain parish contexts, this grandiose minister would not have made it through a trial sermon. But he had once been a highly respected pastor in a conservatively oriented congregation with a long history of obeying "The Pastor," that is, a congregation whose needs for idealizing merger with a mirror-demanding or inclined pastor were strong. In such a narcissistic configuration, a parish's self-cohesion and self-esteem are carried by the idealized clergy, who readily presents himself as their selfobject leader (either via personal narcissistic need or via assumption of the expected idealized role). Reciprocally, the self-esteem and cohesion of the pastor are maintained via the mirroring responses of the parish.

Leadership within this arrangement is focused and clear, namely the person and personality of the pastor as the narcissistically imbued selfobject for the group self of the parish. Such a narcissistic alignment can be strong and durable, but it is always fraught with stress, for each is sensitive to, if not vigilant for, signs that the other is failing to fulfill their assigned narcissistic role. The parish, for its part, is alert to pastoral weaknesses or shortcomings. The idealized pastor is constantly in a position where he is expected to perform successfully. Lay leaders and lonely widows look to the idealized pastor as one whose strength, warmth, or guidance should be made constantly available, and whose personal attentiveness they expect promptly and cheerfully.

The "fishbowl" existence ministers complain about often comes from the pastor being incorporated by parishioners as their elevated—thus scrutinized—selfobject. At times, congregations are attracted to pastoral candidates who manage to sell themselves in spellbinding ways, only to find later that the candidates' grandiose presentations are defensive covers for tenuously structured self-esteem. In any case, no one falls any harder or farther than the once heroic leader.

The grandiose pastor, while at times proudly assured

of his invulnerable place in the congregation, is also sensitive to any sign of criticism or loss of control. If the pastor's needs for grandiose mirroring are of an archaic nature, or his self-cohesion easily threatened, disagreements with him will be met with private and/or public rebukes of those who have dared disrupt the church he heads. Reassurances are sought from lay leaders and staff members in order to fortify both his position as well as his shaken self-certainty. Pastors with vulnerable grandiose selves often use the imagery of "the wolves," who are always at their door, or always ready "to bite you in the ass when you're not looking."

One idealized but injury-sensitive pastor intoned, "If I don't stay strong, there are those in the church ready to crucify me." While this narcissistic configuration holds potential for church growth and community service, the often unseen struggles can become seriously debilitating for both pastor and parish.

"C": IDEALIZING PARISH—ALTEREGO PASTOR

Some pastors are primarily motivated by alterego self-object needs. Congregations, therefore, represent the possibility for strengthening or rectifying the defects in the pastor's self via the normalizing and belonging-affirming presence of others who the pastor takes as being like unto his or her self. In this context, a minister who relies heavily upon alterego relationships may appropriate parishioners as "friends" who are to echo and validate the minister's personal and social being.

Here the lines of distinction between pastor and parishioner tend to be blurred in the pastor's narcissistic construction of his world, for intense alterego relationships are essential in order to counteract the pastor's sense of self-doubt and isolation. Thus, for example, a minister may insist that everyone call him by his first name, and he them by their first names. Worship may be designed to create an informal, intimate, "family" atmosphere. In social settings, such as wedding receptions, the pastor may "let his hair down" by drinking, telling off-color jokes, flirting, or some other action expressing psychologically relinquishment of his set-apart pastoral role. One pastor's intense alterego needs resulted in a rationalized style of ministry where he regularly joined patrons of a local bar for beer, bets, and banter.

Such behavior, however, becomes disappointing and irritating to a congregation bent on being served by an idealized-imaged pastor. Standards for the clergy's character and conduct exist publicly and in the communal unconscious of the parish group self. While the pastor seeks a congregation of cohorts (alterego selfobjects), the parish seeks an elevated, idealized figure. As a result, the pastor tends to have difficulty enacting the traditional pastoral role (he cannot present himself, or allowing himself to be appropriated, as the parish's idealized selfobject leader), and the congregation has difficulty allowing the pastor to be human (they thwart his efforts to elicit alterego affirmations of his unique style and manner of being "me").

The leadership needs of pastor and parish often conflict, based upon this underlying narcissistic pattern of relating. Administratively, the pastor may operate from a "priesthood of all believers" stance. The congregation is made one with the clergy, wherein all share with the pastor similar responsibilities, tasks, and ideals. Much of the pastor's effort may be directed toward getting the congregation to enact this mutual priestly role, for to carry it by himself, or to feel as the set-apart, primary leader, is experienced as alienation and loneliness.

The idealizing-hungry congregation, however, is inclined toward following a strong, wise, experience-endowed pastor, whose task it is to provide guidance and executively to manage the parish's programs. Incompatible selfobject longings and divergent leadership expectations give rise to the expressions of narcissistic depletion and rage with which we have become familiar.

"D": GRANDIOSE PARISH—IDEALIZING PASTOR

Congregations of any size can be structured primarily around the grandiose-mirroring sector of their group self. Here the pastor is expected to be a mirroring selfobject of the parish's own espoused programs and policies. That is, he is "their" pastor, and rather than initiating his own ministering style, the pastor is required to approve of, carry on, and be an exemplary embodiment of the values and visions of the congregation.

In more archaically formed congregations, the pastor's professional and personal actions are to function as enhancers of the parish's grandiose self. Any accrual of public recognition by the pastor is taken by the congregation as their own mirroring acclaim, similar to the way narcissistically disturbed parents garner unto themselves the praise of others when their sons or daughters star in sports.

At times, the selfobject appropriation of the minister takes the form of unempathic disregard for the pastor's personhood, as when a church council constantly reminded their pastor that she was "just a hired hand here." Archaic grandiose oriented parishes, such as the "second-best" congregation we met in the Introduction, may expect their pastor to join them in their history of narcissistic grievances, be a channel for the venting of their rage, and fulfill their desire for community prominence.

A pastor whose narcissistic needs are for merger with an idealized parish self may initially experience renewed vitality as he joins with the self-assured congregation, parallel to the way the well-being of an idealizing-hungry parish soars on being merged with a charismatic, strength-exuding pastor. Potentials for disillusionment are high, however. The pastor's lack of a solid inner core of vitality and firm self-esteem, and his reliance upon idealizing self-object responses for the maintenance of self-cohesion, curtail his ability to serve intensely as a mirroring selfobject.

Furthermore, demonstrated idealizing needs may portray the pastor as a weak or "needy" figure in the eyes of the congregation. For a grandiose self, whether group or individual, not just any figure can be incorporated as an empowering selfobject. That figure must be perceived as imbued with narcissistic specialness. The idealizing hungry pastor may thus fail to enact the character as well as the role of the desired mirroring selfobject.

The grandiose parish tends to offer minimal support for the pastor's pressing selfobject hopes, especially as the congregation becomes disillusioned with the pastor as its mirroring selfobject. As a result, the parish may quickly mobilize to remove the pastor, while the pastor feels powerless to effect any control over his professional fate.

One minister was given 5 minutes to defend himself after 20 parishioners took 5 minutes each building a case for why he should be told to leave. The frustrated words of a denominational leader merit thoughtful attention here: "Those churches with a grandiose self are the hardest of all to minister to." Many pastors would agree.

"E": MUTUAL GRANDIOSE NEEDS

The classical clash between a pastor and a parish is based upon a narcissistic configuration in which the grandiose-mirroring needs in each are central and volatile. To describe the situation as a "power struggle" is to oversimplify and perhaps misdiagnose the psychological process. It is quite normal for pastors and parishioners to have disagreements over certain goals or practices. Efforts to effect the ascendancy of one's goals or practices may even lead to anger toward the other who is blocking the way toward fulfillment of those desired ends. But the other, in this psychological relationship, is still acknowledged and responded to as a person with a separate and right-endowed existence, and anger or assertive action toward that individual continues only as long as that individual is a barrier to the achievement of one's goal.

In the narcissistic clash between a pastor and parish, however, where both are driven by the demand for mirroring recognition and acclaim, the goal is the total ascendancy of the self, in which the other is expected to adhere to, if not applaud, the decisions of the self, and where, when narcissistic rage is elicited, hurt, resentment, and revenge wishes continue toward those who have dared challenge and affront. Self-righteousness tends to characterize the attitude of each, and efforts to win support from others for one's position is common. As a result, competing factions often arise within the church.

When this type of narcissistic conflagration is rampant in a congregation, denominational tactics for quelling such a conflict are often ineffectual, primarily because the narcissistic dimensions of the struggle go unrecognized. Increased communication, clarification of goals, and strategies for implementation, for example, are appropriate for parties who basically perceive each other as individuals in their own right, and are frustrated with each other only insofar as the other is a barrier to the achievement of particular goals. These approaches do not work when the goal is the ascendancy of the self, retribution for injuries suffered, and the establishment of an faithful mirroring milieu.

"F": GRANDIOSE PARISH—ALTEREGO PASTOR

The grandiose-mirroring congregation may respond in a variety of ways to its pastor, whose central selfobject function is to enhance the self of the parish. As indicated above, the parish may be proud of their pastor's accomplishments, which reflect well on them. They may even boast of being able to attract and keep theologically or culturally renowned pastors. At the other extreme are the appropriations of the pastor as merely a utilitarian entity serving the grandiose group, such as when a female pastor was reminded by the parish that "You are here to take care of us, and not we to take care of you."

Midway between these may be the employment of the pastor as but a "resource person," whose assigned role is implementation of the congregation's entrenched programs. Here the pastor's personal involvement, or even spiritual leadership, are not considered of prime importance.

A pastor whose main narcissistic yearnings are for alterego connections will suffer in this parish context. Spouses of such pastors are known to attend other churches, and pastors and spouses in this context often seek friends completely outside the church, if not the town. The pastor's wish for parishioners to act as his "friends," for example, or his efforts to treat parishioners as family peers, are met with cool tolerance, at best. The competency of the pastor may not be questioned, but his ministering style may be resented and rejected by the parish.

Disappointment and rage on the part of the alterego pastor erupt at the flawed, unempathic responses of the congregation. Transference of these reactions to other parish settings is inevitable to some degree. Ministers with archaic demands/needs for selfobject responsiveness, however, tend to transfer their narcissistic rage at a particular parish to *all* parishes, as evident in the often heard derision that "all churches are alike." This phenomenon of generalization arises as a regressive, disintegration product of a narcissistically disturbed self, as witnessed in the fragmentation of the Rev. David F.'s self.

"G": ALTEREGO PARISH—IDEALIZING PASTOR

There are parish selves whose dominant selfobject needs are alterego in nature. Congregations with strong ethnic backgrounds not only exhibit a natural alterego connectedness among members, but may actually strive to retain and protect that homogeneity. Narcissistic enhancement of the group self via mutual alteregoing also occurs in congregations who define their selves according to well-structured theological, financial, or denominational characteristics. Whatever the feature, the alterego structured congregation expects to experience their pastor as one like unto themselves.

This dynamic often determines the acceptance or rejection of a pastoral candidate. Even when phrased kindly, such as, "She'd feel uncomfortable here," the underlying sentiment is often "She's not our kind of people." And should a pastoral candidate pass the alterego test, the alterego forged parish continues its process of reshaping the pastor in its own image, as in the case of the congregation who financially compensated their new pastors in a manner that would allow them to buy quality homes such as the parishioners were accustomed to, and would feel comfortable visiting. While this may seem enviable, such remuneration also included shaping the way pastors and their spouses were to socialize and present themselves.

The possibility for belonging, and the sense of strength which the pastor perceives in an alterego firm parish, may be responded to with eagerness by the idealizing needy pastor. Indeed, the merger-longing pastor may actually possess those personal, cultural, or theological characteristics necessary for inclusion. If the minister does not, however, the pastoral terrain can be extremely rough. Strong alterego bounded parishes can respond with icy aloofness or blatant rejection when pastors are not of their ilk. This unfortunate match often happens when neither pastor nor parish have a decisive say in the placement process.

A single, new pastor with a severely fragile self-structure was open to placement anywhere as long as it was in a metropolitan area. Not only had he grown up "a city boy," but he needed to be in an area that allowed him to "date" and find a mate. Psychologically, he needed an expanded environment in which to find idealized individuals and groups for the maintenance of his self-cohesion, and in which a plenitude of activities could help ward off his fears of dissolution.

His first assignment was in a desolate area in a far northern state, where he was suspiciously received by the parish for being "single and a city boy." He could not make social entries, and no one presented themselves as the self-saving idealized figure he so desperately needed, especially then. More than one evening was spent in secret solitary drunkenness.

"H": ALTEREGO PARISH—GRANDIOSE PASTOR

One generalized alterego expectation articulated by many congregations is the need for the pastor to be "down-to-earth." However vague or nonspecific this may sound, there is a definite alterego yearning here—for the pastor to feel with, be touched by, and show acceptance of the particular life-circumstances of parish members.

One rural congregation specifically asked their bishop to inform the new pastor that he was to wear jeans as his daily dress. In this context, a pastor's successful ministry is carried in large measure by his identification with the inner and outer life of the parishioners. Indeed, an alterego congregation may attempt to elicit and accent the minister's personal side, ignoring or playing down his "pastoral" identity.

This particular alterego requirement of a parish stands to be thwarted by a grandiose-leaning pastor. A preacher's son once related to me that he had never in his life seen his father dressed in anything but a business suit. This mirror-demanding pastor operated similarly in his church. He habitually failed to provide the warmth and personal self-exposure that his congregation needed (and his son as well). He could not accommodate himself to his parishioners, could not respond as their empathic alterego. His attempts to use sermon illustrations familiar to his congregation, who were mostly farm families, came out contrived and somewhat condescending. His "bedside manner" was formal and educative, rather than sensitive and uplifting.

The small rural church was glad to have a pastor, but confided among themselves that they could not really confide in the minister. The pastor psychologically existed on whatever acclaim he could elicit from the parish, but restlessly searched for "more fertile fields" of ministry.

A strong alterego formed parish and a grandiose-inclined pastor often clash, especially when the congregation senses that its way of life is threatened by an innovating, iconoclastic minister. Many southern white churches rejected the efforts of their liberal pastors to open their ecclesiastical doors to blacks. Liberal northern churches resist the proselytizing efforts of theologically and politically conservative clergy. Ethnic congregations are known to thwart efforts of pastors to change celebration ceremonies, or to install other-language worship services. Some churches deprive of their offices those who deviate too far from Canon or covenantal law. Within our religious systems there are many ways to "write off" those who are an affront to our narcissistically perceived world.

"I": MUTUAL ALTEREGO RELATING

In this narcissistic configuration, both pastor and parish are driven by strong alterego needs. The specific characterological features of these needs may not match precisely, or may be incompatible. The latter was evident in a peculiar situation in which the pastor's self required an alterego milieu of energetic, enthusiastic parishioners, while the parish considered itself inexorably moving toward death, calling upon the pastor to serve as their (alterego) chaplain during the dying process.

Various types of alterego alliances exist, for better or worse. One form is represented in those church settings in which the identity boundaries between the pastor's personal and professional self have been realigned, with the pastor defined more as an alterego member than as a congregation's spiritual leader. Another form is manifest in those religious bodies where the functional boundaries between the pastor's role and the parish's role have been blurred or intentionally removed. Here, tasks, responsibilities, and leadership are shared or actually interchanged. An extreme form of alterego alliance is evident in those regressive situations in which pastors and parishioners lose themselves in an enmeshed relationship, wherein they become emotionally dependent, financially intertwined, or sexually involved.

Alterego relating, of course, is not only normal, but indispensable to effective ministry. Distortions arise when the alterego needs are of an archaic nature, which have detrimental effects on both pastor and parish. One minister related how the church became his "real family" when his wife died. Eventually, however, he realized that "the church and I got too much personally involved, and neither one of us was growing, developing, and doing the things we should." Finally, narcissistic rage or withdrawal are just as possible and potent when alterego selfobjects thwart the self as when mirroring or idealizing selfobjects inflict narcissistic injuries.

We have been focusing primarily in this chapter on patterns of narcissistic struggle between pastors and parishes when each is structured around an entrenched narcissistic core orientation. While the specific manifestations of these narcissistic struggles will vary from situation to situation, the underlying dynamics remain functionally similar. Although each narcissistic configuration provides the possibility for the rise of narcissistic tensions, the specific pattern of narcissistic interfacing between congregation and clergy does not in itself automatically lead to ecclesiastical difficulties.

Obviously, there are pastors and parishes who demonstrate instances of these narcissistic configurations, and do well in ministry together. The difference is that they operate out of adequately cohesive selves, where selfobject needs are not so archaically grounded that pastor or parish cannot make use of one another as compensating selfobjects; and where internal narcissistic resources are not so impoverished that pastor or parish cannot endure the inevitable tensions and disappointments in their relationship. Our concern, however, has been with the narcissistic struggles of pastors and parishes.

We turn finally now to broad self psychology informed approaches by which their individual and group selves can be strengthened and restored.

Chapter 6

TOWARD RESTORATION OF SELVES

The descriptive effort throughout these chapters has been to demonstrate how the struggles of pastors and parishes are based on underlying narcissistic tensions, injuries, and regressions. Clergy and congregations whose self-cohesion lacks firmness and whose self-esteem is vulnerable, are prone to respond with degrees of rage and/or depletion when their pressing narcissistic needs are thwarted by unempathic selfobject figures. The overarching therapeutic goal throughout these pages has been to provide an orienting psychological framework that expands the range of our empathic observation, deepens our empathic understanding, and informs our empathic responses to the selves of pastors and parishes. Consequently, clinical, ecclesiastical, literary, historical, and anecdotal illustrations have been intended to give a "feel" for the narcissistic orientations and selfobject expectations/demands of struggling ministers and churches. This final chapter contributes to our descriptive effort and therapeutic goal by considering in broad fashion the processes by which pastor and parish selves can be restored.

Although we have discussed numerous clinical instances of narcissistically disturbed pastors, we will not explicate how clergy can be restored through the process of self psychology informed psychotherapy, or by self-informed pastoral psychotherapy. Many ministers certainly require a long-term psychotherapeutic relationship sensitive to the dynamics of the self. Various pastors alluded to in previous chapters could not have maintained personal integration without it. The therapeutic results of psychotherapy often prove beneficial not only to the self of the pastor, but to the parish self as well—analogously to the way that a parent's regained self-cohesion contributes to the well-being of a child or a whole family's unfolding self. The development of the pastor's self, we have come to see, is not only a personal issue but a professional one as well.

Parishes, as group selves, however, cannot receive psychotherapy, and the pastor who reads these pages does not expect to become an expert on self psychotherapy either as a means for personal growth or for parish development. However, while a narrow analysis of self-restoration via the process of psychotherapy has limited usefulness here, the insights gained from and the healing approaches used within self-informed psychotherapy can be fruitfully applied in a broad way for the renewal of pastor and parish selves, as we shall discuss in a moment.

Although we have also encountered numerous examples of narcissistically disturbed parishes, we will not attempt to explicate the restoration of parishes from the perspective of self-informed pastoral counseling. How the self of the parish, or the selves of parish groups, individuals, couples, and families can be strengthened by self-informed pastoral counseling is of tremendous importance.[1] This approach, however, primarily positions the pastor as counselor to the parish, when in fact the pastor may be a prime reason the parish self is in a state of stress. Furthermore, in a strict sense, parishes do not formally counsel their ministers. Discussing the restoration of selves through the ministry of pastoral counseling would fail to give parishes the guidelines and orientations needed in order to respond empathically to their pastors. Later, however, we shall see how a form of pastoral counseling, namely pastoral consultation, may contribute to the well-being of both clergy and congregation.

But pastors and parishes can experience renewal of their selves in the broad religious-human context of pastoral care, in which each ministers to the self of the other. Pastoral care implicitly contains the recognition that a parish can and is responsible for ministering to its pastor, as well as the reverse. We will consider the process of restoration from this context of ministry in its widest form, namely pastoral care. Here it is more appropriate to offer guiding principles relevant for the many relationships in which pastoral care of selves is practiced.

Heinz Kohut fostered restoration of selves outside the clinical setting. While he clearly distinguished the "cure" of disordered selves in the psychoanalytic setting from the general restoration of selves through nonanalytic means, he intentionally expanded his self psychology framework beyond the clinical context so that it could be applied to wider arenas where selves are nourished and maintained. This was part of the reason that Kohut urged me and others to "translate" his self psychology insights into ways that could be appropriately utilized in our own fields of endeavor.[2] That is what we are now doing as we "translate" dimensions of the curative process in self psychotherapy to the broader process of restoring pastor and parish selves in the context of pastoral care.

Psychoanalytic self psychotherapy is based generally upon certain processes. These are empathic attentiveness to the self's subjective, inner world; empathic observation and understanding of the self's selfobject needs, narcissistic vulnerabilities, and various ways of maintaining self-cohesion and self-esteem; and sustained empathic responses to the self's grandiose, idealizing, or alterego words and actions. In addition, there are acceptance of the self's appropriation of an reliance upon the therapist as selfobject; and empathic explanations and interpretations regarding narcissistic transference, the impact upon the person's self-development from faulty or absent selfobjects, and the self's reactions of rage and depletion in the face of current and past narcissistic injuries.

The overall establishment of a reliable path of empathy between the self and the self's selfobject therapist becomes gradually internalized. That is, they are made part and parcel of the self's inner structure, whereby the person's self-cohesion becomes more firm, selfobject relationships develop in mature ways, primary narcissistic needs are either directly met or filled in by compensating satisfactions, and the self's capacities for empathic resonance are broadened. The newly established functions of a self can only be maintained with the continual effort and support of the selfobject therapist. Consolidation of the self takes time. Improvement of the total functioning of the personality comes about through the transformation of narcissism into ideals, creativity, humor, wisdom, and empathy.

There are three dynamics from this self-psychotherapy process that we can hold up as central for the psychological restoration of pastors and parishes. On the one hand, a pastor or parish's disturbed self-cohesion is regained in part by *feeling empathically understood.* The key point is this: Empathy is *the* means by which weak, inadequately structured, or disordered selves are psychologically restored.

On the other hand, the experience of feeling empathically understood becomes concretized for pastors and parishes, preserved within their selves for future use, by *empathic understandings* of their and others' narcissistic

needs. Empathic explanations carry forward empathic experiences and contribute to the regaining of self-cohesion.
The key point here is: Empathic explanations are a central
means by which experiences of being empathically understood become more permanently a part of an individual
or group's self-structure.

Finally, central in reestablishing lost emotional equilibrium in pastors and parishes is the presence and responsiveness of *empathic selfobject figures*. Here, the key point
is: Restoration occurs as a path of empathy is established
between a self and its selfobjects. The availability of nurturing selfobject figures remains indispensable for the
healthy maintenance of a self throughout its life span.
Briefly stated, the psychological restoration of selves comes
about as paths of empathy are opened between self and
selfobject; more specifically, as the establishment of empathic in-tuneness between self and selfobject occurs on
mature adult levels.[3] The overarching therapeutic result
of self-restoration is the development of healthy selves who
are able to respond with broad encompassing empathy to
their own selves and to the selves of others. We begin by
clarifying and amplifying the pivotal role of empathy in
the restoration process.

THE NATURE AND POWER OF EMPATHY

First, empathy is the capacity to think and feel oneself
into the inner life of another person or of a group of persons. In down-home language, it is the capacity to put your
self in the other's shoes. More formally stated, empathy is
a self's reverberating understanding and deep emotional
resonance with the self of another, where the former shares
for a time the psychic reality of the latter.

Employing this capacity for empathic in-tuneness is
how we come to know other selves. Indeed, empathy is *the*

means by which we come to know the inner, subjective world of individual and group selves. When others say what they think or feel, or when a pastor or parish behaves in a certain way, we try to imagine their inner experience, even though it is not open to direct observation. There is no other way by which to gain a resonating grasp of a self other than through the agency of empathy; that is, by introspective attentiveness to our own feelings as we vicariously place our self in the other self's lived world.[4]

We have to work at this. Empathic observation and understanding require sustained immersion into the other's lived world, alterations and refinements of our empathic impressions, the use of thought experimentation and formulations to help deepen our understanding, and humble attentiveness to the feedback of the selves who are trying to share with us who they are. However difficult or imperfect, empathic introspection is the only means for grasping in depth the inner feelings, meanings, and perceptions of a self.

Effective pastoral care of selves is based upon careful and sustained empathic-introspective immersion into the inner life of the pastor or parish. Empathy grounds and informs all our effective pastoral care-giving responses and acts. While various survey instruments may be useful in gathering parishioners' preferences for this or that, or while a pastor's dossier may contain ratings regarding his inclinations for one type of ministry over another, only by empathic observations and understanding can the inner life of that parish or pastor be known. Failing to employ empathy as the indispensable tool of observation and understanding results in debilitating mismatches, such as those cited in Chapter 5.

The depth and power of empathy extends beyond being a capacity for resonance and the tool for observing and understanding the subjective world of individuals and groups. Empathy is also the fundamental mode of human relatedness. Empathy is that powerful, basic psychological bond between individuals by which selves develop and survive. The accepting, confirming, understanding human echo of one self for another is that central and irreplaceable psychological nutriment by which human life is sustained, developing selves unfold in healthy narcissistic ways, and injured and struggling selves are restored.[5]

Consequently, empathy is not a "preface to" or a "necessary condition for" the "real" work of helping others, whether via pastoral psychotherapy, pastoral counseling, or pastoral care. Selves of pastors and parishes are restored and maintained in the actual occasion of being responded to empathically, where a path of empathy is established between the self and its selfobjects. *Employing empathic observation, responding with empathic understanding, and fostering broad encompassing empathy in others constitutes the essence of the restoration of selves.* Empathy is the grace of God by which the selves of struggling pastors and parishes are psychologically redeemed.

Rather than a gift God grants to only a select few, empathy is a normal capacity of healthy self-development. The capacity for empathy develops as the self-cohesion of the individual or group develops, and empathy as a means of observation can be enhanced in average individuals and groups through experience and training. Broad encompassing empathy for others, for oneself, for culture, and for the cosmos represents one of the highest forms of self-development.

The development of this empathic capacity can become thwarted, however, as we have repeatedly noted in those narcissistically disturbed pastors and parishes described above. Unempathic selfobject responses to the self's mirroring, idealizing, or alter-ego needs result in a weakly structured self with little or no inclination for empathy. Pastors and parishes who demonstrate inadequate empathic understanding simultaneously demonstrate an inadequately developed self due to absent or faulty empathy from their selfobject figures.

Fortunately, such individuals and groups can developmentally progress. As archaic narcissistic selfobject needs mature in the light of new, empathic selfobjects, capacities for broad encompassing empathy also emerge. Although certain selves remain chronically disordered and narcissistically injurious to others, the self of an individual or group tends to move toward creative expressions of its inner being, and struggles to live on the basis of higher values and meanings. Remembering this can help sustain us when our empathy for others becomes sorely tried.

How can paths of empathy be established between pastors and parishes? First, and most broadly stated, by having one's actions and attitudes informed by an understanding of narcissistic needs and vulnerabilities. This means, on the one hand, developing a healthy appreciation for the self of individuals and groups: for the self's grandiose-mirroring, idealizing-merger, and alterego desires and demands; for its sensitivities to narcissistic injury; for the self's narcissistic excesses which express desperate attempts to ward off further fragmentation; and for the self's continued efforts to establish and complete its own development when given an actuating selfobject environment.

A pastor's expanded understanding regarding the self may not change the content or form of what he does in his ministry; but it can amplify the meaning and deepen the effect of what is done. A pastor's broadened theoretical grasp of the self expands the pastor's range of observation and understanding, and sensitizes him to the impact and psychological import of pastoral responses. Similarly, whenever a parish begins to understand that individuals and groups are essentially motivated by the maintenance and growth of their selves, and by the living out of their nuclear ambitions, ideals, and alterego relationships, then that parish is more inclined to think of itself as either supportive or as nonsupportive of the maintenance of selves.

On the other hand, being informed by self psychology insights means developing a healthy appraisal of how our actions and attitudes may be narcissistically debilitating to others. This is a difficult undertaking for us clergy. We tend either to be unaware of our actions, or to disavow their meaning. In both cases, recognition of our "failures" is experienced as a narcissistic injury we want to avoid.

A careful appraisal, however, of what kind of attitude our manner of speaking conveys, of how others experience our habitual ways of looking, not looking, or uneasily looking people in the face, or how our bodily movements, restlessness, or sexual aura subtly shape our capacity to be a reassuring selfobject—this appraisal can enhance the well-being of our own selves, as well as the selves of parishioners. New understandings can result in the joy and satisfaction of new creative-productive efforts, which consolidate our sense of competency and compassion. Parish selves, likewise, can experience renewed vitality and inner harmony through alterations of habitual styles and manners which often unintentionally devalue the sacredness of selves.

Restoration of selves, however, is not to be equated primarily with the gaining of new insights, nor with the expanding of consciousness. While words can convey empathy, and while empathic explanations do inform the conscious mind, the essential psychological nutriment by which selves are held together and renewed is reliable, empathic bondedness with selfobject figures.

These narcissistic connections are often established nonverbally. A pastor's empathic understanding of a parishioner's unsettled psychological condition may be communicated by putting his arm around the hurting individual, touching their hand, sitting quietly nearby, or sharing their tears. Or a parishioner may feel strengthened and uplifted by the sound of the pastor's calm and faith-filled voice, where the words slip away but the reassuring tone lingers long in the heart. Or the pastor's smile and warm laughter at a parishioner's pleasantry or joking may nourish the latter's self-cohesion via the pastor's mirroring approval.

A parish's empathic responses to its pastor may likewise be communicated in nonverbal ways. The light in parishioners' eyes and the look on their faces when meeting the pastor can convey to him a felt sense of belonging, of being in tune with the spirit, and in partnership with, a people central to his life.

A parish's empathic response to its pastor's journey through difficult times may be manifest in their continuing to attend church regularly, retaining an attitude of honor and respect toward him, or making sure that salary needs are adequately met. These might not seem like much to pastors or parishes that enjoy the blessings of firm self-cohesion and esteem, but without this milieu of empathic resonance, strong selves weaken, and weak selves deteriorate further. *The selves of pastors and parishes are maintained and restored through the empathic mirroring, idealizing, or alterego responses they receive from each other, as these responses are amplified and made abundant by the rich humanness-sustaining aspects of their religious life together.*

Paths of empathy are also reliably established as pastor and parish thoughtfully recognize that a pastoral act restores a self only if that act is experienced by the individual or group as resonating with their self. The "power" of pastoral acts resides not in the acts per se, but rather in that they are imbued with narcissistic significance (they function as selfobject supports themselves), or in that they are embodied and conveyed by a selfobject figure.

Narcissistic tensions arise, therefore, when a minister imposes historic and/or personally meaningful pastoral practices upon a congregation who experiences them as foreign, if not frightening. The pastoral acts may be theologically "right," but narcissistically "wrong." A weakening of a parish's cohesive religious life may be set in motion by well-intended but unempathic pastoral acts, rituals, or approaches.

Expanding a parish's appreciation of and reliance upon unfamiliar forms of ministry requires an initial phase in which the minister observes and understands the congregation's ecclesiastical narcissistic style, joins in with their religious and social self-sustaining activities, and establishes himself as a reliable selfobject. Some pastoral acts and approaches, however, may never be able to serve as spiritual enhancers for a particularly structured parish. Restoration of parishes is thwarted when clergy employ pastoral practices that fail to resonate empathically with parishes' narcissistic needs and orientations.

The centrality of empathic resonance as the means for self-restoration helps explain, on the other side, why an inappropriate pastoral act may be received as self-affirming. A pastor who felt guilty when his anger at a parishioner in a counseling session exceeded the moral boundary setting, was surprised to see the parishioner respond with obvious relief.

When he asked about this, the parishioner replied, "I've never had the feeling that anyone ever took me or my problems very seriously. You're getting mad at me made me feel you did, and that you were with me."

Although the pastor's action itself was questionable as a standard mode of care, his energetic, involved response unintentionally met the parishioner's need for a vigorous, invested connection with another. The pastoral care *form* was wrong, but the *content* was right. A path of empathy had been established.

The meaning of events to a self is shaped by whether they are experienced as unempathic vis-à-vis the self and its needs, or whether they are experienced as empathically supportive of its mirroring, idealizing, or alterego needs. While a minister or congregation's care of selves should be grounded in careful empathic observations and understandings, rather than centrally grounded in "good intentions," a "loving heart," or "just being myself," we all can be supported by the knowledge that *at times* our "wrong"

pastoral acts can still be experienced as empathically responsive. The crucial point, however, is that the psychological restoration of selves occurs as a self experiences that
it is understood, that it is not alone, and that its surround-
ing (selfobject) world appreciates it, endeavors to protect
and reassure it, and conveys to it that it belongs.

The example above raises the question of the place of
confrontation in the pastoral care of selves. On occasion,
confrontation in one form or another becomes necessary
in the church. From the perspective of self psychology,
however, there is a central purpose for the use of confrontation, which is to protect selves from further narcissistic injury and regression. When pastors and parishioners
encounter members whose archaic narcissistic demands are
so entrenched and so clamorous for satisfaction that they
disrupt the healthy cohesion of congregation and clergy,
some type of confrontation must be initiated. Likewise must
parishes assert boundaries and request accountability of
pastors whose grandiose, idealizing, or alterego needs un-
dercut the self-cohesion of the fellowship.

The same narcissistic aim of confrontation, however,
must be applied to the disordering selves themselves; that
is, confronting rigid or raging selves should be motivated
by the intention to protect these selves also from further
deterioration. To fail to respond to a self's rage or manip-
ulations, for example, is to fail to be empathically responsive to a self whose continuous actions erode all hope for
its own restoration.

Confrontation, however, has limited usefulness. In all
likelihood, narcissistically rageful pastors or parishioners
will not "learn" from confrontation, nor will their self's archaic actions and attitudes become transformed. But if
confrontation is expressed without vehemence or condescension, with a firmness that is empathically considered,
then rage (or depletion) at being confronted will be min-
imized, and an effort will have been made to safeguard a

poorly regulated self from its own expansional, debilitating ways.

One can always hope, as well, that the confrontation will be experienced as a selfobject's empathic regard. In any case, the narcissistically vulnerable or disruptive will always be with us. Rather than react to such persons with our own rage, we can accept them as tragically injured selves with whom we can empathize, and to whom we can respond with enlightened care.

THE EFFICACY OF EMPATHIC EXPLANATIONS

In self psychology informed psychotherapy, the understanding phase (empathic resonance on the part of the therapist) remains incomplete without a phase in which the therapist offers empathically grounded explanations and interpretations concerning the nature and meaning of the person's narcissistic struggles. Verbal explanations lift the self's experiences up into the dimension of the self's conscious mind, and thus allow him to recall and utilize important selfobject experiences during later periods of life. Such explanations broaden and deepen the person's own empathic grasp of his self, and strengthen the person's trust in the reality and the reliability of the empathic bond that is being established between the person and the selfobject therapist.

In short, empathic explanations increase the self's empathic observation and understanding of its own self, contribute to the development of a path of empathy between the self and its mature selfobjects, deepen the self's capacity for empathic resonance with others, and lead to the establishment of firm self-cohesion.

Explanations and interpretations within the church exist on a wide spectrum. A minister may suggest off-handedly that a frustrated member is "just having a bad day." In a counseling setting, a pastor may attempt to calm a grieving widow by explaining that her present state is normal. From the pulpit, the pastor may give a theological interpretation of human suffering. Parishes make interpretations about their histories, identities, ills, and purposes. Formally and informally, congregations analyze the pastor's weaknesses and strengths, moods and marriage, needs and desires.

Within the context of the pastoral care of selves, the primary purpose of explanations is to support, nourish, and restore individuals and groups. Whether the explanations are theological, psychological, or ethical, whether strongly stated, calmly intoned, or intellectually framed, the narcissistic function of explanations is to convey empathy, carry the experience of empathy, and broaden empathy. Explanations that touch the center of the self help maintain bonds of empathy between struggling factions. Furthermore, they curtail the rise of narcissistic rage, which the experience of not knowing often elicits. Beyond this, pastors and parishes are narcissistically empowered by the process of self-discovery, which efficacious explanations foster. Intuitive and reflective endeavors, especially efforts to understand one's self and others, can become important sources of joy and compensation for a depleted self.

Pastors and parishes need to protect their capacity for responding with empathic explanations and interpretations. Within the church, as elsewhere, explanations often serve archaic narcissistic functions. Selves with strong mirroring needs use explanations as means for their own aggrandizement. Merger-hungry selves may employ explanations to protect the specialness of their idealized figures. Alterego rigid selves are known to espouse explanations that support the rejection of those "not like us." Unfortunately, certain interpretations and explanation also represent the most dehumanizing features of narcissistic rage. The persistence of debilitating interpretations that shape attitudes and action within the church stem not primarily from lack of knowledge or poor reasoning abilities, but from entrenched narcissistic states.

After being exposed repeatedly to distorted or abusing statements, even firmly structured pastors and parishes are themselves in danger of regressing. Unable to sustain their equilibrium in the face of these relentless narcissistic injuries, even the best of pastors and parishes may respond with comments and criticisms which aim to psychologically obliterate offending individuals.

Explanations then endeavor to expel. Interpretations attempt to intimidate. Understanding gives way to labeling. Confrontation degenerates into combat. When pastors and parishes deal with disruptive selves, they must be on guard against the eroding of their own cohesion and esteem, where their own selves regress to archaic levels of acting and reasoning. Regardless of how skilled a pastor is in the practice of ministry, or a parish is in theological reflection, unless they are skilled in self-care, wisely attending to the healthy maintenance of their own cohesion, they will be thrown off balance by narcissistically disturbed selves to such an extent that they become ineffectual in ministry. Care of one's self is not sinful but saving.

Pastors' and parishes' explanations foster connectedness between selves by keeping focused on the proper locus of understanding. If the restorative goal of explanations is to create a path of empathy, then explanations are empathic to the extent to which a self feels understood. While a pastoral care giver appropriately attempts to grasp and articulate the subjective inner world of another, the crucial locus of understanding is not "in the head" or "in the heart" of the care giver. Understanding occurs when a caregiver's explanations connect with and carry forward a self's inner experience. Explanations tend to be unempathic within the church when the locus of understanding is misplaced.

Pastors create difficulties in their preaching, counseling, and teaching when they operate as though *their* understanding is the crucial accomplishment. The term "preaching" has developed negative connotations due to pastors who expound the meaning of this or that, the rightness of these or those, based primarily upon the pastor's formulations. The practice of pastoral counseling suffers when clergy dispense with empathic observation and understanding of particular individuals and families while dispersing advise based upon their storehouse of previously acquired explanations. Teaching becomes ineffectual in the church when it is construed as the passing of insights from the pastor to the pew. In a psychological sense, no interpretation is "right" unless it connects with and opens a path of empathy between selves. However, humbling or difficult to assess, a pastor's explanations and interpretations are efficacious, restorative, only when those who hear feel empathically understood.

Explanations will not be perfectly empathic, of course, and individuals rarely feel perfectly understood (although narcissistically disturbed individuals demand perfect resonance from their selfobject figures). *What is crucial for selves, however, is the experience that empathic connections can be reestablished with their selfobjects when lost.* In the midst of narcissistic tensions, empathic explanations help to restore self-selfobject relationships.

When a minister's words upset a congregation, for example, or his counseling interpretations unduly disturb a parishioner, the minister might consider that selves have been narcissistically injured. At this point, the important issue is not who is right or wrong, but how empathic connectedness can be restored. If that pastor's own self-cohesion is firm, perhaps he can find an appropriate time to explain to the injured selves, in a noncensoring, nonpatronizing way, that in this situation he unfortunately has not fully understood and responded empathically to their needs and sensitivities, that in the light of their particular emotional, social, or spiritual perceptions their responses of anger or depressive withdrawal are understandable, and that the ability of the pastor and the parish to overcome the temporary empathic failures between them can result in the establishment of a mature, wise, and reliable empathic bond.

This is not pastoral confession. Rather, it is once again the effort to establish a path of empathy via explanations that express understanding and clarify narcissistic reactions. Neither does this have to be considered pastoral accommodation. The pastor has not acquiesced; he has attempted to overcome a narcissistic estrangement, so that this and other efforts at pastoral care of selves may once again be mobilized.

A pastor's explanations, of course, often will not—indeed, at times, should not—agree with parishioners' views and attitudes. Such divergent explanations promote the development of parish life when they function as "optimal frustrations." Healthy explanations are "frustrating" in that while a pastor may understand what a parishioner feels, and even acknowledge that the parishioner's upset is legitimate in terms of their particular (narcissistic) perceptions, the pastor does not gratify selfobject wishes in a direct way that the parishioner may want. Not only may the content of the explanation be different from that expected/ wanted by the parishioner, but the very act of substituting an explanation for a parishioner-gratifying action is also "frustrating."

Empathic explanations, therefore, attempt to foster reliance upon empathic *resonance* with selfobjects rather than direct *gratification* from selfobjects. Explanations are "optimal," however, in that the explanations are expressed in such ways that they preserve parishioners' self-cohesion and self-esteem, and basically maintain the bonds of empathy between pastor and parish. Without the "frustration" dimension, a self does not grow. Pure gratification leads to stagnation. Without "optimal" concern for a self's gained cohesiveness, growth is lost.

Finally, explanations are restorative within the church when they are based upon experience-near observations and theories. This is not the place to present a full case for the revision of some traditional theological explanations in the light of self psychology's seminal discoveries. In our opening chapter I suggested that the whole notion of narcissism merited theological redemption. Preaching, teaching, and counseling which continues to berate these normal needs as expressions of humankind's innate sinfulness, for example, not only operate from an inadequate psychological base but, more importantly, fail to react empathically to the ubiquitous narcissistic struggles and strivings of parishes and pastors. The way out of archaic narcissism, wherein narcissistic rage and demeaning use of others as one's tools is rampant, is not through the renascence of guilt, where a guilty conscience suppresses narcissism,[6] but through the renascence of empathy, wherein narcissism is transformed.

The world today is peopled not so much with guilty selves as with empty selves, who yearned not so much for a word of forgiveness as for a word of understanding. Empathic explanations contribute to the restoration of pastor and parish selves as they are informed and, when necessary, modified by insights into the nature of narcissism.

THE SUPPORT OF SELFOBJECTS

Optimal empathic experiences with selfobjects eventually become part of the healthy self-structure of an individual or group, as stated in Chapter 2. Selfobject responsiveness in childhood lays down silently functioning regulatory structures which in adult life operate outside of awareness.[7] Self-nurturing and maintaining functions provided by selfobjects are "transmuted" and "internalized" as specific narcissistic capacities of the individual or group itself.

But selfobjects are not replaced by self-structure in psychological development and in restoration. The attention of selfobjects, who, via empathy, attempt to understand and participate in our psychological lives, remains the indispensable emotional experience for human psychological survival and health.

What changes in self-development is the *nature* of selfobject needs and expectations. A developing self moves basically: (1) from archaic needs for direct, immediate selfobject gratification to sustaining reliance on *empathic resonance* with selfobjects in the adult's life; and (2) from the archaic need for the direct presence of selfobjects to sustaining reliance on the *memory of empathic responses* of vitalizing selfobjects.

There is no self-resurrection in the church. No pastor or parish can, by its own efforts, raise itself from the psychological/spiritual deadness that may pervade it. Moreover, no parish or pastor is ever "autonomous," or "self-reliant." A self survives and is maintained in a milieu of real, remembered, anticipated, or fantasized selfobject support, whether human, divine, or inanimate. A healthy selfobject milieu is the psychological precondition of a good life. Fostering healthy selfobject relationships, therefore, leads to the restoration of selves.

All parishes are strengthened when their religious and social structures provide a variety of selfobject supports. Nonthreatened senior ministers facilitate parish stability by allow members to form deep pastoral relationships with other clergy on the staff. The encouragement of strong lay leadership provides the opportunity for parishioners to idealize and identify with lay selfobjects. The development of diverse social, study, and service groups within the church often meet a wide range of alterego needs. And

the creation of an appreciation-and-recognition atmosphere for what is done in the church, instead of only a
spiritual-duty-and-moral-obligation climate for parish
participation, can healthily meet members' normal grandiose-mirroring needs. A parish's restricted focus upon a
single selfobject does not allow for various narcissistic alliances, and may detrimentally focus narcissistic tensions
within the church upon an isolated figure or group.

Some parishes with persistent narcissistic struggles may
regain creativity and vitality as they are helped to mobilize
around compensating selfobjects. We have previously discussed how narcissistic needs can be met by compensating
selfobject responses. A child's depletion in the face of his
mother's faulty mirroring ministrations can be compensated for by father's availability as a healthy idealized selfobject, for instance. Pastors and parishes, likewise, can
overcome trauma and acquire new structure as they find
new routes toward inner completeness through compensating selfobjects.

Here the wise guidance of denominational leaders is
often indispensable. While not thrusting a candidate upon
a parish, denominational leaders should at times make (or
help pastors/parishes make) informed narcissistic distinc-
tions between what an ailing church archaically "wants" and
what they may restoratively "need." Could the grandiose-
driven "second-best" congregation have regained narcissistic equilibrium through the presence of a warm, engaging female pastor, whose personal alterego relating might
have lifted up within the congregation forgotten or unrecognized satisfactions in "just being us" (the joy of alterego relating)? Can St. J.'s depleted alterego self be res-
tructured and restored through the galvanizing efforts of
a self-assured, healthily grandiose pastor who, with empathic firmness and optimally frustrating explanations, establishes worship and service as the center of corporate
life? Those who make or seek staff changes within the

church could benefit by understanding the place and purpose of compensating selfobjects.

A pastor, likewise, may experience a remobilization of his self, or a filling-in of narcissistic deficits, by utilizing the empathic responses of compensating selfobjects. Although in Chapter 5 we accented the patterns of struggle that ensue from rigidly diverse narcissistic orientations, in milder forms such differences might provide a compensating selfobject milieu by which a pastor can regain his creative-productive self. Such compensations may or may not lead to permanent changes in the pastor's (or parish's) narcissistic orientation, but the potential for some alleviation of narcissistic tension, and the possibility for revitalized efforts when savoring long missed satisfactions, are present via new compensating selfobjects.

The cohesion of clergy and congregation is also maintained when they are helped to experience their selfobjects as portable and expansive. It is natural, of course, for individuals to say, "There are certain places where I feel closest to God." Often they mean their home church. It is unfortunate, however, if God's mirroring, idealizing, or alterego presence is restricted, so that God as a divine, cosmic selfobject becomes narcissistically bound to a concretized locality.

Obversely, the supportive selfobject atmosphere of worship (the uplifting music, the company of fellow Christians, and the hearing of familiar scriptures, for example), or the idealized selfobject role of the pastor, are healthily sustaining as they are able to be carried within the self of an individual or congregation and experienced elsewhere.

The difficulties parishes have in making marked changes in parish life, or that uniting parishes specifically have in giving up their own church buildings, often result from congregations' selves having narrowed to where their spiritual hope and emotional comfort are carried only by their familiar routines and places of gathering. This is not to disparage the soothing and uplifting power of familiar selfobject places, rituals, or articles. We all need them. But a maturing self is able to take its cherished symbolic moments with it, be nourished by these memories when alone, and have them added to in other life contexts.

Of course, the self-cohesion of a parish is centrally maintained and restored through the empathy of its self-object pastor. A minister has narcissistic needs that are normal and appropriate. Healthy care of the pastor's self by the pastor is mandatory. Moreover, a pastor cannot be all things to all persons, and archaic selfobject demands by parishioners need to be modified, if not confronted. With all this as a premise, let it be suggested that a minister expresses pastoral care by remaining responsive to the parish's diverse narcissistic hopes and expectations.

First, while the pastor does not encourage egotism or the building up of vain pride, the pastor does speak and respond in such ways as to mirror the congregation's own grandiose self and thus increase its self-esteem. A parish's wishes and efforts to shine in the community, to do something big and dramatic, or to experience its self as one upon whom God has especially smiled, these are to be met with genuine appreciation, rather than with patronizing tolerance.

Furthermore, the pastor refrains from proclaiming or responding to these narcissistic orientations as "sinful," but recognizes them as expressions of a healthily motivated self, or of a self desperately attempting to maintain its own cohesion. In the face of an individual or group's archaic narcissistic needs/demands, the pastor attempts to help them gradually transform these immature structures into internalized, empowering, creative-productive ambitions and goals.

Secondly, while a pastor does not attempt to manipulate occasions so that he will be idealized by the parish, he does attempt to live, work, and worship in such a way as to be an inspiring and reassuring figure for those who need a focus for their idealizing-merger needs. Furthermore, the pastor resists belittling, playing down, or discouraging his idealization by persons or groups. Instead, the pastor understands their narcissistic need, is empathically responsive to it, and attempts gradually to help transform archaic idealizations into the person or group being led and sustained by their own nuclear ideals and values.

Thirdly, while maintaining identity and integrity, the pastor allows himself to respond as a parish's alterego selfobject. Customs, styles, and established rituals are acknowledged as part of the narcissistic vitality of the congregation, which the pastor joins in a spirit of empathic resonance. When alterego bonding is rigid and rejecting, the pastor attempts gradually to broaden the alterego base, where belonging is sensed beyond the immediate group, and where human and spiritual continuity with people of different backgrounds is inwardly and socially affirmed.

In an analogous way, a parish self's pastoral care of its minister entails responding as his selfobject. A pastor normally attempts to appropriate a congregation as a mirroring, idealized, or alterego selfobject. Some congregations show great understanding for and tolerance of their narcissistically needful ministers, especially when they are young and right out of seminary.

One pastor wrote: "It's been 30 years ago right now that I began a ministry in my first large church. The pastor before me was there, and we shared the service together. I still recall my feelings, and I still remember the Scripture lesson I read that included this sentence, 'Forgetting what lies behind, and pressing forward to what lies ahead . . .' There was in that more than a little arrogance, and ego, and a cry for the people now to love me!" He goes on to express wonder at their patience, and thankfulness for their nourishing responses in spite of his youthful, ungainly grandiosity. Churches can be remarkably understanding and supportive. It's what helps make being a minister both rewarding as well as bearable.

The range and depth of a pastor's reliance upon the parish as his selfobject milieu is no more apparent than at specific transition points in the pastor's life, such as at retirement. Pastors who near retirement often experience increased narcissistic tension. Besides financial concerns, retirement occasions the loss of the emotional sustenance that the pastor has relied upon from the congregation, such as being confirmed in vitality and wisdom by the appreciating parish, being uplifted by idealized members, by the idealized value of active ordained service, and being surrounded by the quiet sustaining presence of alteregos, such as friends within the particular church or the fellowship of colleagues still active in the ministry.

We may well imagine the hurt one pastor felt at this crucial time when his consistory tactlessly posted a sign outside the sanctuary doors which said, "Anyone who wants to head up and help with the pastor's retirement party sign below."—or that another pastor felt when he discovered that the church had decided to combine his retirement dinner with a welcoming dinner for the new minister. Churches can be remarkably thoughtless. It's what helps make being a minister both a challenge as well as a burden. Congregations need to become informed about the vital selfobject role they play in their pastors' lives. As group selves, parishes also can expand their range of empathic observation, understanding, and responsiveness.

PASTOR-PARISH CONSULTATION

The pastoral care of selves by ministers and congregations can also be enhanced when they open their selves to structured reflections on the nature of narcissism. One specific way in which this can be done is through a pastor-parish consultation model based intentionally upon the self psychology framework.

The process begins with a pastor or a parish's elected officials requesting a consultation appointment. At times this is done out of desperation; at other times, as an opportunity for growth. On meeting with the persons involved, I first attempt to immerse myself empathically into the subjective inner experiences of the pastor and/or parish. The self psychology orientation places me in a position where I listen to and organize those experiences along lines considered basic to human development; that is, the complex search for affiliation with life-sustaining selfobjects. As I attempt to understand the inner meaning of the pastor and/or parish's story, I pay close attention to their prevailing levels of self-cohesion, their core narcissistic expectations and sensitivities, the current pattern of pastor-parish narcissistic relating, and the occurrences of, and responses to, selfobject injuries.

Following this understanding phase, I attempt to offer empathic interpretations and explanations regarding their selfobject struggles and strengths. Ecclesiastical conflicts and achievements are discussed in the light of the central self-needs we all have. Self psychological terms are used and explained. The diagram on patterns of narcissistic relationships is utilized as a means for enhancing their reflection on their own particular circumstance.

From this evolves specific suggestions for strengthening the selves of parish and pastor. These include recommendations for alleviating present narcissistic injuries, for stemming progressive fragmentation, for regaining lost self-cohesion, or for enhancing their selves' well-being beyond currently achieved levels. Arrangements are then made for follow-up sessions.

Once again, the primary objective here is to open paths of empathy between selves. This consultation approach has no illusions of "curing" ecclesiastical ills, nor of bringing about in-depth transformations of poorly modified self-need. But it does expect to help foster a wholesome, actuating atmosphere where empathy can gradually supplant the archaic demands and expectations of narcissistically struggling pastors and parishes.

REFERENCES

CHAPTER 1

1. Merwald, A. A. Supervision of the psychological self in pastoral education. *Journal of Supervision and Training in Ministry*, 1982, *5*, 167–180.

2. See, for example: Nelson, J. B. *Embodiment: An approach to sexuality and Christian theology.* Minneapolis: Augsburg, 1978.

3. Vitz, P. C. *Psychology as religion: The cult of self-worship.* Grand Rapids, Michigan: William B. Eerdmans, 1977, p. 9.

CHAPTER 2

1. Goldberg, A. (Ed.). *Advances in self psychology: With summarizing reflections by Heinz Kohut.* New York: International Universities Press, 1980, p. 1.

2. Strozier, C. B. Glimpses of a life: Heinz Kohut (1913–1981). In A. Goldberg (Ed.), *Progress in self psychology*, Vol. 1. New York: The Guilford Press, 1985, p. 6–7.

3. Randall, R. L. Soteriological dimensions in the work of Heinz Kohut. *Journal of Religion and Health,* Summer, 1980, *19,* 83–91.

4. While Kohut recognized the particular narcissistic need of a patient and was empathically responsive to it (to grandiose-mirroring needs, for example), Kohut's psychoanalytic treatment of self-disorders is not based on gratification or fulfillment of the patient's narcissistic longing, as the present discussion may imply. The issue of how restoration comes about will occupy us in the final chapter.

5. My original diagrammatic summary of Kohut's work was slightly revised by Kohut himself, and incorporated into an article by David M. Moss entitled, "Narcissistic Empathy and the Fragmentation of the Self: An Interview with Heinz Kohut," *Pilgrim,* Summer, 1976. This present summary represents an extension and revision of that original, based upon Kohut's later conceptualizations.

6. Previously I indicated the edited volumes on self psychology that are now part of the "history" of self psychology. In addition are a vast literature of clinical articles and manuscripts that affirm and amplify Kohut's study into the nature of the self. See the bibliography for a partial listing.

7. Kohut, H. Forms and transformations of narcissism. In P. H. Ornstein (Ed.), *The search for the self: Selected writings of Heinz Kohut: 1950–1978,* (2 vols.), New York: International Universities Press, 1978), (Vol. 1), 427–460.

CHAPTER 3

1. In the clinical vignettes of pastors and parishes used throughout these pages, I have presented the data in ways that will protect the identity and privacy of those I have come to know.

2. Kafka, F. Conversations with the supplicant. In (W. & E. Muir, trans.) *The penal colony. Stories and Short Pieces.* New York: Schocken Books, 1948, p. 14.

3. Kohut, H. *How does analysis cure?* Chicago: University of Chicago Press, 1984, p. 152.

4. Kohut writes that mothers primarily (and traditionally) provide the mirroring responses for the child's self, while fathers primarily (and

traditionally) provide selfobject idealization responses. It is clear from reading Kohut's case studies that fathers also provide mirroring responses to the child's grandiose self, and that mothers also are looked to as idealized parental selfobjects.

5. Hawthorne, N. *The scarlet letter.* Boston, MA: Houghton Mifflin, 1906, p. 191.

6. Central to the disturbance of each minister we have considered is an insufficiently cohesive, enfeeblement-prone self, resulting in the inability of the individual to sustain his own self-coherence, or effect anxiety control, without massive archaic responses from selfobject figures. The sexual and aggressive drive manifestations encountered in Rev. Michael R. and other ministers with self-disorders, therefore, are not fueled by conflicted infantile drives that are being reactivated in certain situations. Sexual and aggressive activities, rather, are secondary symptomatic manifestations of a fragmenting self which is the locus of the primary disturbance.

7. Kohut, H. *How does analysis cure?*, p. 199.

8. Chambers, M. *Leadership,* Winter, 1985, p. 77.

CHAPTER 4

1. Kohut, H. *The search for the self* (Vol. 2) Footnote #21, p. 837–838. Here is one of the first places where Kohut begins a self-psychological focus on the "group self."

2. Kohut, H. *How does analysis cure?* p. 99.

3. The theme that the way a person structures his relationship to a group may be understood as a reflection of the state of his self is strongly indicated in Kohut's correspondence with Erich Heller (Kohut, H. *The Search for the Self* (Vol. 2), pp. 914–927, and in Kohut's personal interviews with me (*Interviews with Heinz Kohut,* Chicago, Illinois, March 22, 1981, April 12, 1981).

4. See the discussion in Chapter 3 regarding primary and compensatory narcissistic structures.

5. Kohut, H. *The search for the self,* (Vol. 1), p. 429.

6. See the discussion in Chapter 2 regarding the grandiose-mirroring sector of the individual's self.

7. See Kohut's discussion of charismatic and messianic figures and groups in *The search for the self* (Vol. 2), pp. 823–832.

8. See the discussion in Chapter 2 regarding "optimal frustration."

9. See, for example: Kohut, H. *The search for the self* (Vol. 2), pp. 620, 635, 833–834.

10. Kohut, H. *The search for the self* (Vol. 1), pp. 455–458.

CHAPTER 6

1. Randall, R. L. & Schlauch, C. R. *Psychoanalytic self psychology and the activity of pastoral counseling.* In preparation.

2. Randall, R. L. *Interviews with Heinz Kohut.*

3. Kohut, H. *How does analysis cure?*, p. 66.

4. *Ibid.*, pp. 82, 175.

5. Kohut, H. *The search for the self* (Vol. 2), pp. 704–705.

6. Lasch, C. *The Minimal Self: Psychic survival in troubled times.* New York: W. W. Norton, 1984, pp. 200, 253, 258.

7. Kohut, H. *How does analysis cure?* p. 170.

SELECTED BIBLIOGRAPHY

Chessick, R. D. The problematic self in Kant and Kohut. *Psychoanalytic Quarterly,* 1980, XLIX, 456–473.

Fitchett, G. (Ed.). Religion and the self psychology of Heinz Kohut: A memorial symposium. *Journal of Supervision and Training in Ministry,* 1982, *5,* 89–205.

Freud, S. Three essays on the theory of sexuality. In *The Standard Edition* (Vol. 7). London: Hogarth Press, 1953.

———. "On narcissism: An introduction." In *The Standard Edition,* (Vol. 14). London: Hogarth Press, 1957.

Gay, V. Kohut on narcissism: Psychoanalytic revolution from within. *Religious Studies Review,* (July, 1981), 7 199–203.

———. Ritual and self-esteem in Victor Turner and Heinz Kohut, *Zygon,* (1983), *18,* 271–282.

Gedo, J. E., & Goldberg, A. *Models of the mind: A psychoanalytic theory.* Chicago: University of Chicago Press, 1973.

Gerkin, C. V. *The living human document Re-Visioning pastoral counseling in a hermeneutical mode.* Nashville: Abingdon Press, 1984.

Goldberg, A. On the prognosis and treatment of narcissism. *Journal of the American Psychoanalytic Association,* 1974, *22,* 243–254.

———. (Ed.). *The psychology of the self: A casebook.* New York: International Universities Press, 1978.

———. (Ed.). *Advances in self psychology: With summarizing reflections by Heinz Kohut.* New York: International Universities Press, 1980.

———. (Ed.) *The future of psychoanalysis: Essays in honor of Heinz Kohut.* New York: International Universities Press, 1983.

———. Ed. *Progress in Self Psychology,* Vol. 1. The Guilford Press, 1985.

———. Ed. *Progress in Self Psychology,* Vol. 2. The Guilford Press, 1986.

Grant, B. W. Fitness for community: A response to Langs and Kohut. *Journal of Pastoral Care,* December, 1984 *38,* 324–337.

Hawthorne, N. *The scarlet letter.* Boston: Houghton Mifflin, 1906.

Homans, P. Introducing the psychology of the self and narcissism into the study of religion. *Religious Studies Review* July 1981, *7,* 193–199.

Kafka, F. In *The penal colony.* (W. & E. Muir, trans.) New York: Schocken Books, 1948.

Kahn, E. Heinz Kohut and Carl Rogers: A timely comparison. *American Psychologist,* August 1985, 893–904.

Kohut, H. *The analysis of the self.* New York: International Universities Press, 1971.

———. *The restoration of the self.* New York: International Universities Press, 1977.

———., & Wolf, E. The disorders of the self and their treatment: An outline. *International Journal of Psycho-Analysis,* 1978, vol. 59, 413–426.

———. *The search for the self: Selected writings of Heinz Kohut, 1950–1978* (Vols. 1 & 2). P. H. Ornstein, (Ed.) New York: International Universities Press, 1978.

———. *How does analysis cure?* A. Goldberg (Ed.), with P. Stepansky. Chicago: University of Chicago Press, 1984.

————. *Self psychology and the humanities: Reflections on a new psychoanalytic approach.* C. B. Strozier (Ed.). New York: W. W. Norton, 1985.

Lasch, C. *The minimal self: Psychic survival in troubled times.* New York: W. W. Norton, 1984.

Lichtenberg, J. D. (Ed.). *Empathy I* and *Empathy II.* New Jersey: Analytic Press, 1984.

————. (Ed.) *Commentaries on Heinz Kohut's How Does Analysis Cure?* Vol. 6, *Psychoanalytic Inquiry.* Hillsdale, N.J.: The Analytic Press, 1986.

Merwald, A. Supervision of the psychological self in pastoral education. *Journal of Supervision and Training in Ministry,* (1982) 5, 167–180.

Moss, D. Narcissism, empathy and the fragmentation of self: An interview with Heinz Kohut. *Pilgrim,* Summer 1976, 4, 26–43.

Nelson, J. B. *Embodiment: An approach to sexuality and Christian theology.* Minneapolis: Augsburg 1978.

Nelson, M. C. (Ed.). *The narcissistic condition.* New York: Human Sciences Press, 1977.

Niebuhr, R. *The self and the dramas of history.* New York: Charles Scribner's Sons, 1955.

Pruyser, P. W. Narcissism in contemporary religion. *The Journal of Pastoral Care,* December 1978 XXXII, 219–231.

Randall, R. L. Religious ideation of a narcissistically disturbed individual. *Journal of Pastoral Care,* March 1976 30, 35–45.

————. Soteriological dimensions in the work of Heinz Kohut. *Journal of Religion and Health,* Summer 1980 19, 83–91.

————. Interviews with Heinz Kohut, Chicago, Illinois, March 22, 1981, April 12, 1981.

————. The legacy of Kohut for religion and psychology. *Journal of Religion and Health,* Summer 1984 23, 106–114.

————. *Putting the pieces together: Guidance from a Pastoral Psychologist.* New York: Pilgrim Press, 1986.

Rothstein, A. Toward a critique of the psychology of the self. *Psychoanalytic Quarterly,* 1980 XLIX, 423–455.

Stepansky, P. & Goldberg, A. (Eds.). *Kohut's legacy: Contributions to self psychology*. Hillsdale, N.J.: The Analytic Press, 1984.

Stolorow, R. D., & Lachmann, F. M. *Psychoanalysis of developmental arrests*. New York: International Universities Press, 1980.

Tolpin, M. On the beginnings of a cohesive self: An application of the concept of transmuting internalization to the study of the transitional object and signal anxiety. In *The psychoanalytic study of the child, 26*. Chicago: Quadrangle, 1971.

———. Self-objects and oedipal objects: A crucial developmental distinction. In *The psychoanalytic study of the child, 33*. New Haven: Yale University Press, 1978.

Vitz, P. C. *Psychology as religion: The cult of self-worship*. Grand Rapids, Michigan: William B. Eerdmans, 1977.

Wolf, E. "Irrationality" in a psychoanalytic psychology of the self. In T. Mischel (Ed.), *The self: Psychological and philosophical issues*. Oxford: Basil Blackwell, 1977.

INDEX